Under Fives –
Alive and Kicking!

Under Fives – Alive and Kicking!

JANE FARLEY, EILEEN GODDARD AND JUDY JARVIS

Illustrations by Richard Warren

A partnership between the Methodist Church
and the National Society/Church House Publishing

The National Society/Church House Publishing
Church House
Great Smith Street
London SW1P 3NZ

ISBN 0 7151 4918 0

Published 1999 by the National Society (Church of England) for Promoting Religious Education and Church House Publishing

Cover design by Leigh Hurlock

Printed in England by The Cromwell Press Ltd, Trowbridge, Wiltshire

Contents

Under Fives – Alive and Kicking!

Under fives are indeed alive and kicking – ready to explore, with their whole bodies, everything which goes on around them. The world, for them, is always interesting, as long as they are given the opportunity to explore and discover for themselves. They have inexhaustible energy, which, if channelled appropriately, enables them to develop a positive, optimistic and creative attitude to life.

Kicking can be seen as, and often is, an aggressive act. It is seen as something negative. But it also has a strongly positive aspect. Kicking against authority is a natural part of growing up, helping young children to develop as individuals in their own right. Aggressive acts can become creative drive, leading to growing maturity and the development of personality.

Children learn through:

- seeing, touching, smelling, tasting, hearing;
- imitating;
- sharing with others;
- experiencing the world around them;
- discovering;
- exploring;
- making mistakes;
- testing people and situations;
- being given time and space;
- having fun.

This is greatly helped by an environment of love and care where ideas are encouraged and secure boundaries provided. Just as all children learn in similar ways so all children begin to learn about God. For this to happen they need to learn in an atmosphere where a loving God is at the centre.

Alive and kicking with under fives

This book, and its partner volume *Under Fives – Alive*, has been written for everyone involved with under fives. It is full of ideas to help young children to learn through their own experience. The topics are all laid out in the same pattern, which aims to be user-friendly. There is something for all those who work and play with young children – in church, at home, in playgroups and toddlers' groups, in nursery and primary education.

Each topic can be 'dipped into' for use in single sessions or can be extended over a number of sessions. The ideas are meant to be jumping-off points for further discovery. Some have obvious links to the seasons of the year, special events and the Christian calendar.

At the heart of every topic is the setting. This is the opportunity for children to explore and discover for themselves. The setting should never be there just to look good (though we hope it will!) – rather, it is meant to be the stimulus to all the rest of the learning. Encourage the children to become involved as they arrive.

Practical hints

The following suggestions are set out in the pattern which is used in each topic:

AIM

Keep the aim clearly in mind. Use it as a method of assessing the effectiveness of the session.

PREPARATION

All the settings and many of the other activities require preparation (and clearing up). Time spent in planning and preparation is essential and is what leads to a stimulating yet smooth-running session. Good relationships with the caretaker are worth cultivating! In some sessions where special preparation is needed, this has been highlighted

SETTING

Don't be daunted by some of the suggestions! Get as many other people as possible involved. Good preparation makes for an easy but effective session. Make the setting children-friendly, where they can relax and enjoy themselves.

SHARING

Use the questions suggested in this section to encourage the children to enter into conversation. This might take place informally or with the group. Follow up with more 'open' questions (ones that do not have 'yes' or 'no' for an answer). Make sure that all the children have a chance to speak, either in the main group or in smaller groups.

Then have a playtime. Encourage the children to use the setting in any way they want to, being interested, but not interfering, in what they are doing.

BIBLE STORY

Make the Bible come alive by building on the experiences the children have had through using the setting and through sharing together. Help them to understand that the Bible is not just a history book but is about real people who have a great deal in common with people today. The Bible story has been written in full as a guide to how it might be told to young children. Helpful hints:

- Settle the children comfortably (preferably on the floor).
- Make sure there is eye contact with everybody.
- Try to tell the story rather than reading it.
- Do not rush.

Remember – stories should be fun, so enjoy telling them. If you won't, ask someone else to do it.

ACTIVITIES

Offer a choice of activities. Encourage the children to work at their own pace, using their imagination. The results may not always be exactly what you had in mind, but the value to the children is in the doing.

MUSIC AND RHYMES

Choose the songs or rhymes which suit the group. Don't worry if there is no accompanist. Remember that music and rhymes can have a very calming effect on excited children.

The *Big Blue Planet* (*BBP*) songbook (published by the Methodist Division of Education, Youth and Stainer & Bell 1995) is suggested as a companion to this book, as it has a number of original songs suitable for under fives. (A cassette tape is also available.)

Use rhymes for fun. Children like rhythm, repetition and the sound of words. Many of the poems and rhymes in the book are tradi-

tional and already known and loved by children. The others are easily learned and, by frequent repetition, help in the development of children's vocabulary.

DRAMA AND MOVEMENT

Children need to be active. The suggestions offer creative ways in which children can be physically involved.

ANOTHER STORY

These stories link the topic to the everyday experience of the children. Don't be afraid to replace them with a story from your own experience. Remember that children are fascinated by new, long words. They will not need explaining if they are used with the right intonation in the right context.

STORY BOOKS

Make a collection of children's story, picture and reference books. Ensure that they are always available in a quiet corner, created by a rug and a few cushions. Is your group registered to borrow a book box from your local library?

WORSHIP TIME

Prayer time is very important. Make sure that it is imaginative and creative. It is essential to help young children to experience an atmosphere of awe and wonder in worship. (It is a great help to have a low table to gather round. Use a chipboard display table, cut down, or an upturned stacking plastic box. Cover with a cloth, changing the colour and texture as appropriate.)

Other ways of using *Under Fives – Alive and Kicking!*

Under Fives – Alive and Kicking! is primarily for those who work with under fives in play-groups, nurseries and church groups for young children. On most occasions children will be in their own room, exploring the world and their understanding of it in their own surroundings. However, there are other times when children are together for which it is possible to adapt some of the material in this book.

Whichever way you intend to use the ideas remember:

●   Know your situation.
●   Find others to share the planning, preparation and participation.
●   Choose your theme.
●   Adapt the material to your particular group.

Pram services

●   Keep the service short, simple and safe.
●   Have things to see, touch and do (with or without the adults).
●   Say or sing an action rhyme.
●   Tell a story.

All-age worship

●   Have a visual display which is the focal point. Do not be afraid to use it, adding to it, taking from it and re-creating it in the context of worship.
●   Use groups to take responsibility for different parts of the worship.
●   Tell the Bible story using simple language and in a way that is suitable for everybody. (People of all ages enjoy stories.)
●   When appropriate use drama, mime, dance.
●   Consider whether any of the activities can be adapted for use. (Even adults enjoy making hand prints if they can feel there is a purpose to the activity, it is well-organized and it is sensitively presented.)
●   Allow everyone the opportunity to opt in or out of activities.
●   Don't limit the songs to those which are suitable for the very young.
●   Try to adapt the prayers for wider use without losing their creativity and spontaneity.

Holiday and after-school clubs

●   Many of the themes can be adapted for a whole week's programme. Activities could be extended to challenge older children.
●   Don't be afraid to build in a quiet time for reflection, awe and wonder.

Primary school assemblies

- The material meets many of the criteria of Key Stage 1 of the National Curriculum.

- It lends itself to the preparation of assemblies by classes and groups, particularly in the infant school.

- The broadly Christian emphasis is balanced by an approach which can also be used in a multi-faith context.

- The assembly theme can be carried back to the classroom for further development within the National Curriculum.

At home

- *Under Fives – Alive and Kicking!* is a user-friendly source of ideas for the parents and grandparents of young children.

- It offers opportunities and ideas for them to share together in conversation and play.

- It gives a wide variety of stories, both religious and secular, which are closely linked to the themes in the book.

- Both children and adults can share the humour and liveliness of the pictures.

Acknowledgements

The authors extend special thanks to Mary Roseweir for all her support.

The author and publisher gratefully acknowledge permission to reproduce copyright material in this publication. Every effort has been made to trace and contact copyright holders. If there are any inadvertent omissions we apologize to those concerned and will ensure that a suitable acknowledgement is made at the next reprint.

A. & C. Black: 'Chop and chip' (p. 99), 'When I'm walking in my red shoes' (p. 11) and 'Tick tack too' (pp. 11-12), in Ruth Sansom, *Rhythm Rhymes*, A. & C. Black, 1964; 'A-hippity, hippity, heigh-ho!' (p. 12), 'Ding-dong! Ding-dong!' (p. 19), 'The rain comes pittering, pattering down' (p. 31), 'There is no need to light a night-light' (p. 75) and 'I knew a man who always wore' (p. 96) in Clive Sansom, *Speech Rhymes*, A. & C. Black, 1974.

HarperCollins Publishers Ltd: 'I love all shining things' (p. 3) by Elizabeth Gould in *Come Follow Me*, Evans Bros Ltd, 1956, 1966.

Hodder and Stoughton Publishers: 'I'd like to build a canoe for two' (p. 27), 'Jill has a triangle' (p. 31) and 'John rides on a bicycle' (p. 87) by Alison Winn in *Helter Skelter*, Brockhampton Press Ltd, 1966. Reproduced by permission of Hodder and Stoughton Limited.

The Methodist Church Division of Education & Youth and Stainer & Bell: 'I like eating' (p. 15), 'I love the crunch, crunch, crunching of the seashore' (p. 23), 'With my hands I clap, clap, clap' (p. 99) and 'God has given us eyes to see, let's look' (p. 99) from *Big Blue Planet* (The Methodist Church Division of Education & Youth and Stainer & Bell, 1995).

National Christian Education Council: 'Here behind the hedge I stand' (p. 79) by M. G. Martyn in Donald Hilton (comp.), *A Word in Season*, NCEC, 1984. Collection copyright © Donald Hilton. Rhyme reproduced by permission of the publishers.

Penguin Books Ltd: 'Find a spark, light the fire' (pp. 16, 95), 'First of all we'll dig a hole' (pp. 35, 67), 'Guess what we're going to buy today' (p. 11), 'I'm going, I'm going, I'm going' (p. 7), 'In the middle of the wood' (p. 79), 'Let's all ride our bicycles' (p. 91), 'Let's pretend to make some bread' (p. 83), 'Let us build a bungalow' (p. 39), 'Look behind you!' (p. 64), 'Pancakes, pancakes for tea' (p. 95), 'Ten golden daffodils' (p. 7), 'Um-pa-pa, um-pa-pa' (p. 87), 'When children are asleep in bed' (p. 67), 'When the smoke begins to rise' (adapted, p. 35), 'When you want to cross the road, cross the road' (p. 91) and 'Writing letters, writing letters' (p. 55), in Linda Hammond, *Five Furry Teddy Bears*, Penguin Books, 1990. Text copyright © Linda Hammond 1990. Reproduced by permission of Penguin Books Ltd.

Scripture Union: 'Sail, sail your fishing boat' (p. 103) by Sheila Clift in *Let's Praise and Pray*, copyright © Scripture Union, 1994. Used by permission.

Ward Lock Educational: 'The man in the moon'(p. 3), 'Today as I went out to play' (p. 59), 'It's funny' (p. 43), 'The aeroplane taxies down the field' (p. 87) in Jan Betts, *Knock at the Door* (Ward Lock Educational, 1980). Reproduced by permission of the publishers.

Abbreviations

BBP   *Big Blue Planet*, Stainer & Bell and the Methodist Division of Education & Youth, 1995

CP   *Come and Praise*, Volumes 1 and 2, BBC Books, 1978

FG   Peter Churchill, *Feeling Good!*, National Society/Church House Publishing, 1994

H&P   *Hymns and Psalms*, The Methodist Publishing House, 1983

HPPA   Harrow Pre-School Playgroups Association

JP   *Junior Praise*, Combined Music Edition, Marshall Pickering, 1986

JU   *Jump Up If You're Wearing Red*, National Society/Church House Publishing, 1996

See the 'Resources' section (p. 107) for full titles of all story books and music and rhyme books. Please note that any songs or rhymes that are printed in full with no source cited have been written by the authors of this book.

Sun and moon

Aim

To use the sun and moon to help the children to develop a sense of awe and wonder in creation.

Setting

If possible, use two separate rooms or use this theme on two separate weeks.

SUN ROOM

- Decorate the walls with suns, cut from deep orange yellow paper or card.
- Sun gives heat: sunbathing equipment – rug, bathing costumes, sun glasses, sun hats, sun cream.
- Sun makes things grow: things growing – plants and flowers in pots, further pots, seeds and compost for planting. Sunflowers.
- Sun gives us light: have all the lights on, making the room as bright as possible.

MOON ROOM

- Decorate the walls with moons, crescent both ways and full moon, cut from lemon-yellow paper.
- Draw the curtains, making the room as dark as possible.
- Stick fluorescent stars to the ceiling.
- Torches of different shapes and sizes.
- A collection of overcoats, anoraks, gloves and scarves.
- Pictures of night creatures – bats, owls, badgers, etc.

Sharing

Where is the sun? What's it like? When can we see it? Why mustn't we look straight at the sun? When can't we see it? What do we see at night instead? What shape is the moon? Why is it different shapes? What can you see on the moon if you look very carefully? Why does the moon look different from the stars?

Use the settings and everything in them to pretend either that is a sunny day, or that it is night time.

Bible story and activity

(or use the Creation story in *Under Fives – Alive*, p.86)

GENESIS 1.16–19

Prepare a large piece of frieze paper, one half blue and one half black. Put the paper up at a level which the children can reach. Have appropriate pictures and coloured paper available for children to tear shapes, creating the story as it is told. Use Pritt stick to fasten the shapes to the frieze.

God made the sun. (Tear out orange circles and glue them on top of each other on the blue half of the frieze.)

God made the moon. (Tear out yellow moon shapes and glue them on top of each other on black half of frieze.)

God made all kinds of animals. (Tear out pictures of different animals. Put night creatures on the moon side of the frieze where possible.)

God made the birds. (Tear out pictures of birds, including owls, for the moon side of the frieze.)

God made fish. (Tear out pictures of fish.)

Last of all, God made people. (Add pictures of people.)

Activities

- Make a sun and a moon collage using foil, sequins, fabric and coloured paper. Alternatively use card and pasta shapes. Spray with metallic paint. NB. This should be done by adults into a cardboard box and in a well-ventilated area.
- Do bubble painting in sun and moon colours on sun and moon shaped paper.
- Use card cut outs in the shape of the sun and the moon at different phases as stencils to spatter paint over.

- Use salt dough to make suns and moons and paint at a later date when dry (see Appendix page 105).
- Make a group-work sun and moon book with alternative coloured pages and pictures relating to day or night.

Music and rhymes

SONGS

'I love the sun, it shines on me' (*Someone's Singing, Lord*) (*Add a verse about the moon.*)

'I like the sunshine' (*BBP*)

'God who made the earth' (*CP*)

'O what a wonderful world' (*BBP*)

'The sun has got his hat on'

'All things bright and beautiful'

'Sun arise, she bring in the morning' (*Tinderbox*)

'Praise him in the morning' (*H&P*) (*Add a verse appropriate to the moon.*)

RHYMES

'Hey diddle diddle, the cat and the fiddle'

I love all shining things –
        The lovely moon
The silver stars at night,
        gold sun at noon . . .
The beauty of all shining things
        is yours and mine,
It was a lovely thought of God
        to make things shine.

Elizabeth Gould in *Come Follow Me*

Through moonlight's milk
She slowly passes
As soft as silk
Between the grasses.
I watch her go
As white as snow,
So sleek so white,
The moon so bright
I hardly know
White moon, white fur,
Which is the light
And which is her.

Douglas Gibson in *Happy Landings*

The man in the moon
Came down too soon
And asked his way to Norwich
He went by the south
And burnt his mouth
With eating cold plum pudding

Knock at the Door

Drama and movement

Encourage the children to become the following shapes: a full moon, crescent moons, a new moon, a half moon and a very big round sun.

Ask them to act out:

how we feel when the sun is shining; what we do when the moon comes out (prepare for bed, lie down and shut their eyes).

Another story

It was the first day of Matthew's holiday to France. It was such a long journey that it was dark when they got to their holiday house and he had to go straight to bed. But he was up very early in the morning, looking out of his window in the bright sunshine. Outside there was a huge field, filled with thousands and thousands of sunflowers. Matthew noticed that they were all looking at the road. Not one was looking his way.

Matthew and his mum and dad went out for the day. When they came back it was nearly teatime. Matthew was astonished when he looked at his field of sunflowers. They had all turned their heads and seemed to be looking at him!

Next morning Matthew had a good look at his sunflowers. They had turned their faces again and were looking at the road. But when he came home they had all turned to look at him.

In the middle of the night he looked out of his window. By the light of the moon he could see that all the sunflowers had dropped their heads as if they were nodding off to sleep.

'Mum,' he said, 'what are the sunflowers looking at? They keep turning their heads round and round!' 'They are looking at the sun,' said his mum. 'As the sun moves across the sky they follow it all day and then rest at night. That's why in France they are called "tournesol" which means turn to the sun.'

Story books

- *Oliver's Wood*
- *See for Yourself*
- *Sun's Hot – Sea's Cold*
- *What Is the Sun?*
- *Whatever Next*

Worship time

Stand by the picture of the creation. Thank God for all the wonderful things in our world. Sing 'O what a beautiful world'.

Flowers

Aim

To use flowers to help children discover the beauty and wonder of the world.

5

Setting

On tables round the room place the following:

- Fresh flowers – the variety will depend on the season.
- Containers – vases, damp oasis, pin holders.
- Flowering houseplants.
- Wild flowers – a limited variety, respecting the countryside.
- Paste pots, herb jars, little jam/sauce jars.
- Garden flowers – in a trough, or garden pots with flowering plants.
- Dry oasis, containers and a selection of dried flowers.
- Baskets, dry oasis and a variety of silk flowers.
- Catalogues and seed packets, garden books and magazines.
- Flower designs on table cloths and printed fabric.

 ## Sharing

What is there in your garden which isn't green? Do you know the names of any flowers in your garden, the park or the window boxes? Where would you go to buy flowers? Why would you buy flowers? What do flowers need in order to stay alive?

Use the items in the setting to make small arrangements.

 ## Bible story

GENESIS 1

This is a story that people used to tell about how they thought God made the earth.

God had a very busy time, everything was dark, so God made the sun. Now there was day and night. Next God shaped the earth. Now there were great oceans, mighty rivers and tiny streams. But the land was brown and bare. 'It needs to have something growing on it,' thought God. 'How can I do that? I know! It needs tiny seeds, and sun and rain to make them grow.'

All kinds of seeds began to grow. It wasn't long before some seeds grew into grasses which stood tall and blew in the wind. Other seeds grew into plants which had many different coloured flowers on them and smelt lovely. Some other seeds grew very tall and strong with branches. These were trees and they had beautiful flowers, pink and blue and creamy white. After a little while fruits and nuts appeared on the trees. The flowers bloomed at different times of the year. Inside each flower new seeds grew. Some grew in little pods. When these dried in the sun the pods popped open and the seeds fell on the earth and started to grow again.

The earth began to look very beautiful with all the colours and God was really pleased.

Activities

- Sow seeds (nasturtiums are fast germinating).
- Make a garden in a tray.
- Make a flower montage from pictures torn or cut from catalogues.
- Make cards sticking dried flowers as a collage.

Antirrhinum and nasturtium,
Rose and columbine.
Anemone and hyacinth,
Broom and dandelion.

Blue lobelia and hydrangea,
Thrift and clematis.
Chrysanthemum and buddleia
What a world it is!

Music and rhymes

SONGS

'God made the colours' (*CP*)

'God made the heavens and earth' (*BBP*)

'All things bright and beautiful'

'Think of a world without any flowers' (*CP*)

'What colours God has made' (*JP*)

RHYMES

Small and round, small and round
The bulb is deep inside the ground.
Stretch and grow, stretch and grow
Up the stalk comes slow slow slow
The buds unfurl, the buds unfurl,
See the petals outwards curl.
Straight and tall, straight and tall
The flowers grow against the wall.

More Word Play, Finger Play

Ten golden daffodils
Dancing in the sun
A naughty dog came running by
and knocked down one.
(*Repeat using the children or fingers – nine,
eight, seven, etc.*)

Five Furry Teddy Bears

Drama and movement

Use the following rhyme:

I'm going, I'm going, I'm going –
Curl up tightly on the floor.
Now I know how it feels to be growing.
Straighten back very, very slowly.
First the tips of my leaves push up through
the ground,
Push hands up gradually until level with chin.
quietly, so quietly, they don't make a sound.
Put finger to lips.

I stop for a rest, then down comes the rain,
Fold arms, then indicate rain with fingers.
my leaves have a drink, then I'm growing
again.
Cup hands and pretend to drink. Continue growing.
If the sun starts to shine, my leaves open wide,
Move arms upwards and outwards.
but when the wind blows they all try to hide.
Clasp arms overhead and sway from side to side.

I've roots at the bottom and leaves on top.
Point to feet then head.
I'm growing and growing, but when will I stop?
Stand up slowly.
Perhaps I'm a flower, a bush or a tree
Use hand to show the different plant heights.
what do you think I'm going to be?

Five Furry Teddy Bears

Another story

'Can I play that game too, Grandad?' Josh asked. Grandad was sitting at the table with lots of small envelopes and he was moving them about, looking at them carefully on both sides and then putting them in a pile. It wasn't really a game. It was a very important job. Grandad was delighted that Josh wanted to help him and he told him to climb up on the chair and he would show him what he could do.

It was a cold wet January day; it was the right kind of day to start thinking about summer and beautiful colours and gardens. Every year Grandad spent January days sorting out the packets of seeds that he would be sowing, some in the greenhouse and some in the garden.

Grandad showed Josh the packets and the pictures of the different flowers. Josh chose the ones he thought would look nice in the garden. He matched the colours and sorted the big packets from the little ones. He helped Grandad sort a pile of all the ones that needed to be planted in the warm, and then the ones that could be planted straight in the garden were sorted in another pile.

When this was done Grandad asked Josh if he would like to go with him to the greenhouse. 'Why is it called a greenhouse?' asked Josh. 'It is all glass and it hasn't even got a green door.' 'Let us look through the glass and see what you can see,' said Grandad. Josh looked and said 'Plants'. 'Yes, green plants,' said Grandad, 'so that is why it is a greenhouse. All the plants have green leaves.' 'It might have been called a leaf house then,' said Josh. Grandad laughed at the joke. 'I think it's time we went planting.'

When they had planted the seeds and covered them up with a thick blanket of soil they went indoors. Grandma had lots of magazines on the table which was covered with newspaper. 'What are you doing, Grandma?'

asked Josh. 'Waiting for you to help me make a flower garden,' she replied. Josh didn't understand but Grandma soon explained that they would cut pictures of flowers from the magazines and catalogues and stick them on to brown paper. They worked hard. Josh enjoyed finding pictures and sticking them on the soil-coloured paper. It wasn't long before he was calling Grandad to come and see the lovely garden he and Grandma had made.

Story books

- *Flowers*, 1994
- *Flowers*, 1992
- *Let's Look at Flowers*
- *Sunflowers*
- *Why Do Sunflowers Face the Sun?*

Worship time

Place a basket of flowers in the centre of the circle of children and surround it with some of the things the children have been doing in the activity time. Thank God for flowers, for their different colours, for their lovely smell and the way they make our world more beautiful.

NOTE

Be sensitive to the fact that not all children will have window boxes or gardens.

Boots and shoes

Aim

To help children, through the focus on boots and shoes, to explore feelings.

Setting
EVERYDAY SHOES

Children's and adults' shoes of different types, sizes and colours, including trainers, slippers, high-heeled shoes, sandals, mules, plimsolls, ankle boots, knee-length boots, wellington boots, Doc Marten's, babies' shoes.

SHOES FOR SPORTS AND HOBBIES

Any of the following: football boots, cricket boots, golf shoes, trainers, ballet shoes, tap-dancing shoes, riding boots, walking boots, ski boots.

SHOES FOR TOYS

Shoes of different kinds for Barbie, Action Man, and the toys to go with them.

FOOTWEAR

Skis, roller skates, skates, roller board, flippers, horseshoe, galoshes, waders.

SHOE ACCESSORIES

Shoe horn, shoe stretcher, shoe last, shoe tree, shoe polish (neutral), brushes, dusters.

Sharing

What do we wear on our feet? If it's wet, what do we wear? If it's snowing what do we wear? (Use other examples as appropriate.) Who doesn't wear shoes? Why not? What are your

favourite shoes? What kinds of shoes do you wear for doing different things, e.g. in the house, going to a party, going to school, on holiday? Why is it important that shoes fit properly?

Give the children plenty of opportunity to try on the different kinds of footwear, which should lead to imaginative play.

Bible story
EXODUS 3.1–15

Moses was feeling lonely and very sad. All his family and their friends were far away in Egypt. They were also very unhappy. The king of Egypt, Pharaoh, had made them into slaves. They had to do everything he said and he made the other people in Egypt be cruel to them as well. Back at home in Egypt Moses had got very angry with Pharaoh – so angry that he got in great trouble and had to run away.

So, here he was, feeling lonely and very sad. He was looking after some sheep in a wild place. It was bare and rocky with just a few bushes and a little grass for the sheep to eat.

Away in the distance Moses could see the great mountain, Horeb. He decided to take the sheep there to find something to eat. It took a long while to get to the mountain. The sheep kept wandering all over the place but in the end Moses managed to get them there. They started to climb the mountain.

After a while Moses and the sheep stopped for a rest. The sheep wandered off to find something to eat. Moses was tired. He sat down for a rest. He was still feeling lonely and very sad.

Suddenly, he saw a very strange sight. Nearby him a bush was burning, but the branches and twigs weren't turning black. The bush went on burning. The flames were orange and yellow but the bush stayed green and fresh. Moses thought, 'What a strange thing! I must have a better look.' He went up very close to the bush. Then he heard a voice. The voice called, 'Moses, Moses!' Moses was astonished. 'Here I am,' he said. The voice spoke again. It said, 'Don't come too close. Take off your sandals. The place where you are standing is special, it is holy ground.'

Trembling and frightened, Moses took off his sandals. The voice came again: 'I am God, the God of all your people. I know how sad and unhappy your people are, so I have a job for you. You must go back to Egypt. You must see Pharaoh. You must bring the people out of Egypt.'

Moses was astonished. 'What me?' he said. 'They'll never believe me!' 'Yes they will,' said God. 'I will be with you. Tell them that I sent you and that I will bring them out of Egypt to a new life.'

Moses wasn't feeling lonely and sad any more. God had a job for him!

Activities

- Shoe and boot printing (see Appendix page 105).
- Do rubbings of the bottoms of shoes.
- Draw round shoes of different sizes and shapes. Cut out the shapes and use to make a montage.
- Practise tying up shoes, using lace boards or adult shoes.
- Use shoe laces to make patterns in card which has punched holes.

Music and rhymes

SONGS

'When I'm feeling down and sad' (*BBP*)
'Rabbit ain't got' (*Apusskidu*)
Substitute verses:
Rabbit ain't got no shoes at all,
Just some furry paws.
Rabbit ain't got no wellies at all,
Just some furry paws.

Guess what we're going to buy today
from a shop not far away.
Guess what we're going to buy today
Some (ballet shoes) to (dance) in.

Substitute other verses:
Football boots to kick in.
Leather boots to walk in.
Big tough boots to climb in.
Trainer shoes to run in.
Army boots to march in.
Slippers soft to creep in.
Wellie boots to splash in.
(*Sing to the tune of 'Here we go round the mulberry bush'*.)

Five Furry Teddy Bears (adapted)

RHYMES

Walking in my red shoes,
Down the busy street,
Walking in my red shoes,
Whom do you think we'll meet?
'Hello, Jane.' (*Children greet a friend.*)

Repeat with different kinds of footwear, meeting different children.

Rhythm Rhymes

Tick tack too,
Mend a lady's shoe,
A red shoe, a red shoe,
Tick tack too.

Tick tack too,
Mend a baby's shoe,
A white shoe, a white shoe,
Tick tack too.

Tick tack too,
Mend a horse's shoe,
An iron shoe, an iron shoe,
Tick, tack, too.

Rhythm Rhymes

A-hippity, hippity, heigh-ho!
Away to the blacksmith's shop we go.
 If you've a pony
 That's lost a shoe,
 You can get her another
 All shining and new –
A-hippity, hippity hop!

Speech Rhymes

Drama and movement

Mime skating, swimming with flippers, skiing, skate-boarding, playing football, ballet dancing, tap-dancing, etc.

Another story

Bhanu was crying in the cloakroom when Mrs Reed found her. 'Whatever is the matter, Bhanu? It's time for dancing. Why are you crying?' Bhanu was crying so much she couldn't tell Mrs Reed what was wrong.

She had come to school that morning with her shoe bag with her new dancing shoes in it. She had hung it on her peg and now it wasn't there. She did love her new shoes and her pretty shoe bag with the Teletubbies all over it.

Mrs Reed found a tissue and mopped up Bhanu's tears and Bhanu told her the sad story. 'Oh don't get so upset. We will find them. Shoes don't walk far without their owners, you know. Let's look in here first to see if they have fallen under any of the lockers.' They looked at one end and then the other and just as they were looking at the other end Bhanu started to cry again. 'What will my mummy say? She only bought the shoes yesterday and she told me they cost a lot of money. It was my special shoe bag that my nanny had made for me.' She cried again.

'Mop up those tears. You can't look through them. Everything looks blurred.' Bhanu sniffed and wiped her eyes and as she bent down on the last side to look for them, in through the door came Sam swinging the Teletubbies over his head.

'Look what I've got!' he said. 'Someone's silly shoe bag, it had fallen into my bag.' 'It's mine,' said Bhanu 'and it's not a silly shoe bag.' She sounded cross but Mrs Reed reminded her to say thank you to Sam for bringing it back. Off she went to her lesson, skipping along in her new dancing shoes.

Story books

- *Alfie's Feet*
- *Getting Dressed*
- *Shoes*
- *Sonny's Wonderful Wellies*
- *Two Shoes, New Shoes*
- *Whose Shoes?*

Worship time

Gather together for prayer. Tell the children that in some places when people talk to God they take their shoes off like Moses did. Ask them all to take off their shoes. Say prayers for people who are sad – because they are lonely, worried or frightened.

Vegetables

Setting
ON THE WALLS

Display pictures of vegetables obtained from a greengrocer or cut from magazines.

ON TABLES IN DIFFERENT AREAS OF THE ROOM

- *Root vegetables* – potatoes (new and old), turnip, swede, beetroot, carrots, parsnips, onions, etc.
- *Salad vegetables* – lettuce (of various kinds), tomatoes, cucumber, spring onions, radishes, white cabbage, celery, etc. (Have some sliced up for tasting.)
- *Vegetables which grow above the ground* – cauliflower, brussels sprouts, cabbage, runner beans, peas in pods, broccoli, asparagus, mushrooms, leeks, garlic, etc.
- *Cooked vegetables* – mashed and diced potato, chips, crisps, potato croquettes, potato waffles, mashed swede, diced turnip, fried onions, tinned tomatoes, mushy peas, baked beans, sliced mushrooms, sliced leeks. (Provide plastic spoons for trying.)
- *Other vegetables* (if appropriate) – sweet potatoes, gourds, artichokes, fennel, yams, etc.

Encourage the children to explore vegetables by looking, touching, smelling, tasting and eating.

Sharing

What name do we have for all the things on the table? Which ones are your favourites? Are there any you like? Can you match the cooked vegetables with the right uncooked vegetables? What vegetables did you eat yesterday? Which ones are made of potato?

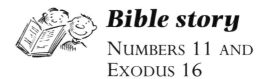

Bible story
NUMBERS 11 AND EXODUS 16

'We're going on a journey. Isn't it exciting! I wonder where he's going to take us. It's wonderful to have escaped from Egypt.'

The people of Israel had been very unhappy in the land of Egypt. At last, the great leader, Moses, had helped them to escape. There were thousands of people, with all their sheep and other animals, so they moved very slowly indeed.

At first, it all seemed exciting. It was wonderful to have escaped from Egypt. But the journey went on and on. It went on for months and months. There was no food and the people began to grumble. 'Have you brought us here to starve?' they asked Moses.

Moses spoke to the people. 'God answers all our need,' he said. 'Every day, when you get up in the morning, you will find white flakes on the ground [looking a bit like snow, though it doesn't snow in that part of the world]. Collect up enough for your family for the day. Grind it between stones to make flour and then use it to make a kind of bread. We shall call this food manna. You mustn't be greedy, you must only take enough for the day. You must trust that God won't let you starve.'

Next morning, when the people woke up, they found the manna lying on the ground. They had to collect it quickly, for when the sun came up it melted away. With it they made bread to eat. Some people didn't trust that God would send the manna every day. They collected enough for two days. When they got up in the morning they discovered that the extra manna was full of worms and smelt horrible! They soon learnt their lesson!

But after a while the people began to grumble again. 'We're not starving,' they said, 'but we're fed up with this manna. It's boring. We remember the wonderful food we had in Egypt. We had cucumbers and leeks and onions and garlic. It would have been better to stay in Egypt. Manna is boring.'

Moses was also fed up. He had a hard job and he was angry with the people for being so ungrateful. But, soon, his problems were solved. A great crowd of birds, called quails, landed on the camp. There were thousands and thousands of them. The people were very excited. They killed the quails, cooked them, and ate far, far too much. After months of eating no meat they began to feel very, very ill. Moses did not have to explain to them. They knew that if they were going to get to the place where God was leading them they must learn to trust God to look after them.

Activities

- Do vegetable prints using dryish, thick paint and vegetables cut in half. Use paint on a piece of sponge on a tray. If possible include a small cut cabbage for its spectacular pattern.
- Make coleslaw (see Appendix page 106 for recipe).
- Make a salad using lettuce, tomatoes, spring onions, etc.
- Make soup in a pressure cooker or microwave.

- Make a collage of vegetables using magazine cuttings.

Music and rhymes

SONGS

'I like eating' (*BBP*) (*Use the following verse to replace the first verse.*)

'In my little garden' (*Apusskidu*)

'I'm very glad of God' (*Someone's Singing, Lord*)

I like eating (*echo*)

Brussels sprouts and swede (*echo*)

Chips and cabbage (*echo*)

Food is what I need (*echo*)

Leeks and baked beans (*echo*)

Onions and green peas (*echo*)

Thank you God, for food.

Adapted from 'I like eating' (*BBP*)

God made the leeks to grow,

God made the leeks to grow,

All things were made by God,

God made the leeks to grow, etc.

(*Sing to the tune of 'A-hunting we will go', holding up each vegetable in turn and singing the appropriate words.*)

RHYMES

'Five fat peas in a peapod pressed'

(Word Play, Finger Play)

One potato, two potato, three potato, four,

Five potato, six potato, seven potato, more.

(Play the game with a partner, each putting a closed fist on top of the others' fist.)

Traditional

Find a spark, light the fire.

Watch the flames getting higher.

Brr, it's cold!

Ouch, it's hot!

Let's put (carrots) in the pot.

Put in one, put in two.

Now what else have we to do?

Stir it fast!

Stir it slow!

Who would like to have a go?

Five Furry Teddy Bears

Drama and movement

Act out the story of the Enormous Turnip as the traditional story is re-told.

> An old couple wanted to grow a turnip.
> First they had to prepare the ground:
> *(Dig the ground, rake it, scatter the seed.)*
> They watched it grow from a tiny shoot to an enormous turnip.
> *(Grow from being curled up seeds into being huge turnips.)*

The old man tried to dig the turnip up.
(Everyone digs as hard as they can, to no effect.)
The old man grasped the top of the turnip and pulled as hard as he could
(Choose someone to be the old man.)
The old man got his wife to help.
(Choose someone to be the wife, to hold him round the waist and help him pull.)
They still could not do it.
The farmer called the children one at a time.
(Add children to the back one at a time and try to pull it out each time another child is added.)
A little mouse came into the garden and saw what was happening and offered to help. He held on to the back person and they pulled and they pulled and all of a sudden the turnip came out.
(Everyone pulls the turnip and as it comes out they all fall backwards.)

Repeat if you wish, using other children.

Story books

- *The Gigantic Turnip*
- *The Trouble with Grandad*
- *Vegetables*

 # Worship time

Ask each child to bring a piece of vegetable and to put it in a large pot in the middle of the group. Ask someone to add some water from a jug, and another to add salt and pepper. Thank God that we have plenty of food to eat, made from tasty things. Pray for all the people in the world who never have a good meal.

Bells

Aim

To explore the part bells play in everyday life and religious traditions.

Preparation

Have two pomegranates available, one cut in half, ready for the Bible story.

Setting

MUSIC

● Church bells.

ON THE WALLS

● Bells of different sizes cut out of silver and gold paper.

ON A TABLE — BELLS TO LOOK AT

● Brass, china or glass ornamental bells.
● Christmas tree decorations.
● Wedding card/invitation with bells on it.
● If possible, silver bells from cake decorating shops as used on wedding cakes.
● Clock with a chime.
● Picture of Big Ben.

IN THE CENTRE — BELLS TO HANDLE AND PLAY

● Percussion instrument bells.
● Handbells.
● Cow and goat's bells.
● Small bells from pet shops or craft shops.
● Hanging door chimes.
● Alarm clock, kitchen timer.
● Bells from morris dancers.
● School bell.
● Ship's bell.
● Old-fashioned bell for calling attention.
● Bicycle bell.

Encourage the children to use the setting and everything in it to discover the sounds of different bells – for a limited period!

Sharing

(Make sure the music is still playing.) What can you hear? Where are there some near here? What are they like? (Look at the picture on page 17.) What do you do to make them ring? What kinds of bells have you got in your house? Where else do you use bells? Look at, and talk about any special bells you have.

Bible story

EXODUS 28.33–35 AND 39.22–26

'Are you ready for the gold thread yet?' Abner asked. He and his sister Tabitha were watching their father do some special sewing. They liked to sort out the long coloured threads and choose their favourites. Abner's was usually one of the really bright red threads. Tabitha always liked a very deep purple one. The gold threads were very precious, so they were kept folded together in a piece of cloth.

Their father said, 'I've just got this one pomegranate to finish sewing before I start on the next part of the pattern. Can you find me some scarlet thread for this last piece?'

His needle, with its trail of scarlet thread, went in and out of the blue cloth. It was stretched on to a big wooden frame and he was sewing a pattern along the edge. The pomegranates looked quite real. Some of them showed the outside of the fruit. Some showed the dark red seeds. 'Now, I think I can start on the bells, that go between each pomegranate,' he said, 'so I'll thread my needle with some of the gold thread.' 'Why do you always sew a pattern of pomegranates and bells?' asked Tabitha. Her father explained that his job was to make special clothes for the priests in the Temple in Jerusalem. 'This pattern has always been used on the priests' robes,' he said. 'It's there because, a long time ago, our people were wandering about, looking for a good place to live in. One day they found a spot where lots of pomegranates were growing. They decided to settle down there and we are here still!'

Soon he had stitched a gold bell between two of the fruits and started on another one. 'Now, on the hem of Aaron's robe – he was the first person to be a chief priest – real little golden bells were sewn,' he said. 'That meant that people could hear him moving even when they couldn't see him. He was the only priest who could go into a special part of the Temple, called the Holy of Holies.' He explained that all the robes that priests wore had bells sewn into the pattern, to help people remember Aaron, the first chief priest.

'I think bells and pomegranates make a beautiful pattern,' said Abner, 'and now I know why you sew them.'

(*If you think it would be helpful, have a pomegranate ready to show at the end of the story.*)

Activities

- Make a bell collage using red, purple and gold paper or materials.
- Make bell-shaped biscuits (see Appendix page 105).

- Print with bell shapes, using potatoes, foam or a string block (stick string in a bell-shape to a block of wood).

Music and rhymes

SONGS

'Frère Jacques'

'Jingle bells, jingle bells'

'We all march to the beating drum' (*BBP*) (*Second verse* – 'We all play on the ringing bells')

'The Bell of Creation' (*CP*) (*verses 1 and 4*)

'Long ago, prophets knew' (*H&P*) (*choruses 1 and 4 only*)

RHYMES

'Ding dong bell, Pussy's in the well'

'Oranges and lemons'

'Pr-r-r' says the door bell when the visitors call
'Br-br' says the telephone bell in the hall
'Ting' says the bell on the big London bus
'Clang' says the fire engine 'Make way for us'
'Ping' says the station bell 'train won't be long'
But the bell on the steeple says 'Dong, dong, dong'.

Anon

Ding – dong! Ding – dong!
All the bells are ringing.
Ding – dong! Ding – dong!
Ringing all the day.

Speech Rhymes

Drama and movement

Give as many children as possible a bell of some kind which can be shaken (take turns if necessary). Move round the room slowly, ringing the bells gently. Gradually speed up, ringing the bells more vigorously as you do so.

Shake the bells low down and high up. If you have different bells at different pitches shake the low bells low down and the high bells high up (having identified which is which).

Another story

'Everything ready, lads?' shouted Bill. 'Then we're away. Cast off please, Tom, and steer straight ahead, Pete.' The three men were setting out early in the morning, from Deal, for a day's fishing. Their boat, called the 'Merry Maid', was loaded with all the gear they would need to catch cod and sole and plaice. They planned to sell the fish in the market the next day.

It was a lovely morning, with a clear blue sky and just a few fluffy white clouds around. 'Should be a nice trip today in this lovely weather,' said Pete. 'Hope it's a good one for catching fish as well.'

Tom was soon busy sorting out the huge piles of fishing nets with their bright orange floats. When they reached the place where there were usually big shoals of fish, these nets would be tossed over the side of the boat to catch them. Then, later on, the men would haul the nets back on to the boat to see what their catch was like.

It was Pete's job on the boat to keep a sharp look out, using his eyes and ears. The sea near Deal is very busy indeed, with lots of big cargo ships and car ferries crossing the Channel. There are plenty of smaller boats too: fast motor boats that whiz through the water and graceful yachts that seem to skim over the waves and other fishing boats as well.

There are no road signs out on the sea, but each ship or boat, however big or small, has to keep to certain rules so they don't crash into each other. Today was really clear though and Pete could see all the other boats and ships. People on the smaller ones often waved to each other as they passed. Sometimes they shouted 'Ahoy there!' That's the way you say 'Hello' when you are at sea.

There wasn't usually so much waving and shouting from the big ships. Their way of saying 'Hello' was with a very loud 'Hoooooot'. 'I'm sure they are telling us to get out of their way,' Bill used to say to the others.

Soon, the 'Merry Maid' was at the best fishing place. It is called the Goodwin Sands because there are great sandbanks there just under the water. Fishermen have to be very careful not to get stuck on these sandbanks. They know that it can be dangerous.

Bill, Tom and Pete worked really hard, until the huge boxes on the deck of the boat were full of fish. 'Time to be off now, if we want to get home before it's dark,' said Bill. 'We've had a good day's fishing.'

Suddenly the blue sky turned grey and it was much colder. Then, it seemed from nowhere, came the fog, rolling over them like a thick blanket. They couldn't see anything beyond the edge of the boat. Sailors and fishermen hate fog. It makes them feel as if they are lost.

Pete, who had really sharp ears said, 'Thank goodness we can hear the hooters on the other ships and the "Boing, Boing, Boing" from the Varne lightship warning us about the Goodwin Sands. It's behind us, so we must be going the right way,' said Tom.

Sure enough, the 'Boing, Boing, Boing' got fainter and fainter as they chugged on. Soon they were landing at Deal. 'Safe home, thank goodness,' said Pete. 'Thank goodness for that bell too.' The others agreed.

Story book
- *Jingle Bells*

Worship time
Listen to the tape of the church bells ringing. Talk about when the bells ring – for church, for weddings, for funerals. Pray for people who have been happy this week, then for people who have been sad.

Stones

Aim

To use stones to remind children that they have choices. Many things in our world, including stones, can be used for good or bad purposes.

21

Setting

Set out five trays:

TRAY 1

Very tiny stones (as in fish tanks) with tea-spoons and small containers, e.g. lids of aerosols.

TRAY 2

Small stones and pebbles (shingle) with larger spoons, short lengths of plastic water pipe, plastic flower pots and other containers, e.g. yoghurt pots, bean cans.

TRAY 3

Beach pebbles and other stones in a variety of sizes.

TRAY 4

A selection of fruit cut open to show the stones, e.g. apricots, peaches, avocados, dates, prunes, plums, nectarines, mangoes.

TRAY 5

Semi-precious and precious stones – costume jewellery, rings, brooches, beads, etc.

Also – a collection of things which live under stones. Pictures or examples of snails, slugs, earwigs, etc.

Sharing

Where do you find stones? What do they feel like? Where have you been to see lots of stones? What does it feel like to walk on stones? What are they used for? Why do we have to be careful with stones?

Explore the setting and everything in it.

Bible story

1 SAMUEL 17.40

'Who's going to go out on the hills to look after our sheep if you go off to join the king's army?' Jesse was quite worried when his son Eliab said he didn't want to be a shepherd any more.

It could be quite dangerous to be a shepherd in the lonely places where the sheep wandered to find fresh sweet grass. There were high rocks and steep slopes and sometimes a sheep climbed up them and then couldn't get down again. A shepherd would have to get up there somehow and maybe carry the sheep back. He would have to be a very strong person and a good climber. The other danger could be from wild animals like wolves and lions, which might try to catch a sheep or lamb to eat.

Eliab's brothers Abinadab and Shammah were shepherds too but they really needed three of them to look after the sheep properly. 'How about David becoming a shepherd? He is only young but he is very strong,' said Eliab. 'I'm sure he'd soon learn how we do it.' David was their youngest brother, who had just finished going to school. Jesse wasn't sure about young David being a shepherd, out by himself sometimes, with all those dangers. 'We'll ask him,' said Jesse, 'and see what he says.'

David was quite excited when his father talked to him about learning to be a shepherd. 'I'd really like to be out there, climbing steep rocks and fighting off bears and lions with my big strong stick,' he said. His brothers laughed when they heard this. 'It's not that easy, you know David. We've all had to learn about looking after sheep and the best way to frighten off the wild animals.' Jesse agreed David could have a go, but he'd have to stay close to the other two until he had learned what to do.

First of all Abinadab took David with him up the rough stony paths that led up on to the hills. He showed David how to pick out the smoothest way as he walked in front of the flock of sheep. 'If it's very rough,' he said, 'the sheep can get sharp stones stuck in their hooves and then you have to stop and get them out.'

Then Shammah said, 'Come down to the stream with me and I'll explain how we choose the best stones to use when we want to chase away any wolves or lions that get near the sheep.' The shepherds used a strong piece of cloth, called a sling, to swing round and round with a stone inside, before letting go of one end. The stone would whiz through the air very fast and give an animal a nasty blow. David picked out some big stones with jagged edges. 'These look good,' he said. 'They are heavy enough to knock out an animal.' 'Oh no!' said his brother Shammah. 'Rough stones might get caught in the cloth, so we choose the very smoothest ones we can find, not too small or too big, then they'll fly through the air.' After some practice, David became really clever with his sling; in fact he was soon a very good shepherd.

 ## Activities

- Paint pebbles. Coat afterwards with PVA or lacquer.
- Use some stones to build walls with ready-mix cement. If possible, go outside for this!
- Outside, turn stones over to see what is underneath, replacing the stones afterwards.
- Make an indoor garden with stones, soil and plants.

 # Music and rhymes

SONGS

'Only a boy called David' (*JP*)

I love the crunch, crunch, crunching of the seashore,
I love the crash, crashing of the sea,
But the thing I like the best, the very, very best, is to know that God loves me.

Adapted from 'I love the pit, pit, patter of the raindrops' (*BBP*)

I'm so glad that God made stones.
God made stones, God made stones.
I'm so glad that God made stones,
Thank you God.

I'm so glad that God made pebbles, etc.

I'm so glad that God made rocks, etc.

I'm so glad that God made cherries, etc.

(*Sing to the tune of 'London Bridge is falling down'.*)

Turn over a stone, turn over a stone,
What can you see? What can you see?
I thought that I might find a mouse,
But all that's there is a little woodlouse,
I think I might have disturbed his house,
I'll put it back.
(*Sing to the tune of 'Three blind mice'.*)

RHYMES

'I had a little cherry stone' (*This Little Puffin*)

Come and see what I've got here,
My special smooth black stone.
I found it on the beach last week
When we were coming home.
It lay there among the shells
Very near the sea.
Gleaming in the sunshine

Just waiting there for me.

I'm going to build a rockery
please help me move this stone.
It's so very heavy
I can't do it all alone.

Drama and movement

Mime the following: lifting large stones, skimming stones, building walls, scrambling over huge stones, walking on pebbles by the sea.

Another story

'Gran doesn't know that Helen can walk now, does she?' said Greg. 'Won't she be surprised?' The family were on their way to stay with Gran for the weekend. She had just moved into a new house and they were all wondering what it would be like. Greg was especially excited about Gran's new garden. He knew it would be different from the garden at Gran's old house. That garden had been good for football and riding bicycles. What would this new one be like?

'Well, I hope there's a flat part that Helen can walk on safely,' said Mum. 'She can't manage steps and slopes very well.' 'Not yet,' laughed Dad, 'but it won't be long!'

Gran was standing at her door to welcome them. 'I'm so pleased to see you all here in my new home,' she said. 'You're my first visitors.' In they all went, through the hall into a lovely sitting room that had glass doors opening on to the garden. 'Sit down,' said Gran. 'We'll have a drink and then I'll show you round.' Greg finished his drink quickly. He could hardly wait for the others to finish theirs and Helen seemed to take ages. Then Mum put her down on the floor. She stood up and was off, walking straight out into the garden. Gran was surprised and delighted. 'She's a

good little walker already,' she said. 'I think we'll follow you and you can see the garden first. That's what you want, Greg, isn't it?'

Mum seemed a little bit worried. 'Is it safe out there for the children?' she asked. 'I can hear water splashing.' 'Come and see,' said Gran. 'It's quite safe.' She led the way out into the garden. 'I wanted some water in my new garden, but I thought a pond would be dangerous with a little one like Helen around, so instead I've got a pond of stones.' There outside was a low brick wall, built in a circle, like a little round pond. It was full of big, smoot, stones, gleaming in the sun as the fountain in the middle splashed on them. There was something else too. Helen had pulled off her shoes and socks, climbed on to the little wall, and she was sitting under the fountain, getting soaking wet. They all laughed. 'She's safe enough,' said Dad, 'but very wet!' Greg decided to join Helen. 'I think you're very clever, Gran,' he said. 'I like your new garden already.'

Story books
- *Bathwater's Hot*
- *Crystal and Gem*
- *The Pebble in My Pocket*
- *Rocks and Minerals*
- *The Snow Lady*

Worship time

Ask each child to choose a stone, bring it to a central place and together build a cairn. Remind the children that travellers on journeys build cairns to let people know they have passed that way. The cairn in the middle reminds us that God is with us wherever we go and whatever we are doing.

Say a prayer asking God to help us to use the things he has trusted to us to help people, not to hurt them.

Wood

Setting

NATURAL WOOD AREA

Branches, twigs, logs, slices of trunk, natural strange shaped pieces of driftwood from sea - shore and land.

WORKING WITH WOOD

Planks, dowelling, beading, various off-cuts, rough wood, sanded wood, sand paper, sawdust, wood shavings, a plane with the blade covered.

POLISHED WOOD

Wooden bowls, boxes, small wooden table, jewellery, fruits, eggs, candle sticks, beeswax or wood polish, dusters, building bricks.

PAINTED WOOD

Decorations, photo frames, toys, Russian dolls, bookends, coat hooks, door plaques, small brush.

UNPOLISHED WOOD

Wooden spoon, chopping board, pot stand, cooking tools, garden dibber, rolling pin, brooms.

Sharing

- Holding a piece of polished wood in your hand, ask where wood comes from.
- What kinds of things do we have at home made from wood?
- Look at a piece of cut trunk and ask what the ring patterns are.
- Feel a piece of unplaned wood and talk about the feel. Compare with a piece of polished wood and ask what the difference is.

Bible story

1 KINGS 5.3–6, 9–11

At last! Solomon thought. Nobody is at war with us, there is peace and maybe I can do what David, my dad, always wanted to do. There were always wars or threatened wars while David was King and he was always trying to keep his people safe from harm.

Solomon sent a messenger to Hiram, who was King of Tyre, telling him what he wanted to do. Hiram was the only person Solomon knew who could provide him with enough workers and the right wood for this special job.

Solomon said he would pay Hiram back whatever it cost if he would help him carry out his father David's wish. Hiram was excited to be able to be part of the job. He'd thought King David was a very special person.

The job began. Ten thousand workers each month worked with stone and wood, cutting the trees, hewing the stone, sawing the wood and making it smooth ready to be taken to the place where Solomon and his team of workers were planning to build this special house.

It was an enormous house with lots of very, very big rooms and a winding staircase. The stones were built up to make the shape of the house and then every wall inside and outside was covered with the beautiful wood from the cedar tree. The floors were all covered with wood from the fir tree.

Some of the wood was carved carefully to look like flowers, angels, fruits and palm trees and these were used to decorate the walls and ceilings. There was not even a small piece of stone to be seen. It was all covered with wood.

When all the woodwork was finished it was all covered with gold and it looked fantastic. This very special house had taken seven years to build.

Solomon and Hiram were delighted with it and said that they were sure King David would have liked it too. They called it the temple.

Activities

- Sand blocks of wood with sand paper.
- Make collages with lolly sticks, twigs, cocktail sticks, wood shavings and sawdust.
- Build with wooden bricks.

Music and rhymes

SONGS

'Peter hammers with one hammer' (*This Little Puffin*)

This is the way we measure the wood
Measure the wood
Measure the wood
This is the way we measure the wood
When we are making a table.

This is the way we saw the wood, etc.

This is the way we sand the wood, etc.

This is the way we put it together, etc.

This is the way we polish it all
When we have made the table.

(*Sing to the tune of 'Here we go round the mulberry bush.'*)

RHYMES

'Here's a tree with trunk so brown' (*This Little Puffin*)

I'd like to build a canoe for two
With a seat for me and a seat for you.
We'll need some wood
That's bendy and good,
And a big pot of waterproof glue.
We'll have to use
Copper nails and screws,
And canvas for making the skin.
And while you're fixing the outside on
I'll be fixing the inside in.

I'd like to build a canoe, would you?
It really shouldn't take long to do.
If only we had
Some tools like Dad.
I wish he would help us too.
Perhaps you could bring
A plane sort of thing,
While I draw a careful plan.
I'd love to build a canoe for two,
And, what's more, I'm certain we can.

Helter Skelter

Drama and movement

Pretend to:
Chop down trees.
Chop up logs.
Saw the wood.
Hammer the wood.
Plane the wood.
Paint the wood.

Another story

'Look what I have found!' called Simon to his mother who was walking a little way ahead of him along the beautiful stretch of white sand. 'It is too big for me to pick up. I need your help.'

His mother turned round and could see that Simon had a very big grey object in front of him and he was trying to lift it. 'I'm coming,' she said. 'Don't hurt yourself. What a beautiful piece of wood.' 'Where has it come from?' said Simon. 'There are no trees along the beach.' 'How do you think it got here?' said his mother, and Simon started to guess. First he thought perhaps someone had dropped it from a lorry, but there were no lorries on the beach. Then he had the crazy idea that a bird might have dropped it, but it was too big for any bird to pick up in its beak. Perhaps it blew through the air in a strong wind. 'I don't think it could have been any of those,' said his mother. They had a close look at it and it was damp and grey and in the knobbly parts there were small pebbles and even a small shell. 'Has it been in the sea?' Simon asked. His mother said she thought it had. 'But how could it have got there?' asked Simon.

As they sat on the sand beside the piece of wood his mother explained that there is not a sandy seashore everywhere. And in some places the seashore is by tree-lined hills and the wind sometimes breaks pieces from the trees. They fall in the sea and are then carried for miles in the water, because wood usually floats. If the sea gets very rough sometimes the wood comes near the shore and it will be brought in on a big wave and be thrown on to the beach or the sand. The sea waves go down and leave the wood on the sand. They remembered that it had been windy the previous night and that was probably how the wood had come on to the sand.

'Can we take it home, please?' asked Simon. 'It will fit in the plastic shopping bag you brought for collecting treasures.' Mummy agreed, and they picked it up and put it into the bag.

'You know who would like this,' said Mummy. 'Uncle Ken, because he will clean it with his metal brush and then polish it for you and you can have it on the book case in your bedroom to remind you of our seaside discovery.' Simon thought that was a great idea but he asked if he could take it to Playgroup first to show them what he had found.

Story books
- *Big Book of Noah's Ark*
- *My Dad Is Brilliant*
- *The Trunk*

Worship time

Invite the children to collect a wooden object or some natural wood from the setting and sit, in a circle, on the floor around a central worship display. This display can be on a wooden tray and could contain a piece of branch, a log or cross section of tree trunk, some sawdust and wood shavings, and a cross made from wood.

In the prayer thank God for trees which give us shelter, for trees that give us wood which can be made into so many things and for giving us Jesus who died on a cross of wood.

Rhythm

Setting

COLLECTION OF MUSICAL INSTRUMENTS

Tambour, tambourine, drum, cymbals, maracas, castanets, bells, marimba, triangle, etc.; beaters and drum sticks.

COLLECTION OF THINGS TO MAKE RHYTHMIC SOUNDS

Home-made instruments:

- Squash bottles with grit, rice, peas inside.
- Metal tins with plastic lids, hit with spoon, piece of dowel, etc.
- Washing-up liquid bottles with filling.
- Milk bottle tops on a string.
- Pieces of wood to hit with wooden spoon, piece of dowel, etc.
- Elastic band round open box.

RHYTHMIC TAPES BEING PLAYED

Jazz, rock, reggae, classical, heavy metal, etc.

ON THE WALLS

Pictures of drums and other instruments.

A REAL DRUMMER

Bring in a real drummer – don't worry about doing much else!

Sharing

Start by clapping the rhythm and saying the name of each child. Put some music on and clap to the rhythm, then tap feet to the rhythm. Introduce the word rhythm. Listen to a clock ticking. What other sound patterns can you think of? (Heart beating, cuckoo, dog barking, horses' feet, police and ambulance sounds, washing machine.)

Enjoy the setting and everything in it.

Bible story
1 CHRONICLES 15.16

'I think we are nearly ready,' said King David. 'We are going to have a wonderful parade to bring the Ark up to Jerusalem.'

The Ark was a very special thing that the people had carried round with them for many, many years. It was a wooden box with a beautiful gold lid. It had a long pole at each corner so it could be carried on people's shoulders. Inside it there were some very important papers, all rolled up.

Now King David had found a good safe place where the Ark could be kept. It was a large flat piece of rock on top of a hill. A huge tent had been put up to shelter the whole place. The king sent messages to all the people in Jerusalem to say that the new home for the Ark was ready. He told them that the next day would be a holiday for everyone and he hoped they would all come and join the parade.

Samuel and Miriam were very excited when they heard this. 'Can we go and join the parade?' they asked their mother. 'Oh yes,' she replied, 'your father is one of the men who have been asked to play the music for us all to march to. Uncle Zechariah and your cousin Asaph are playing music too, so we are all going.'

The children got up very early the next morning, so they could watch their father get his lyre ready. He kept it wrapped up in cloth and looked after it very carefully. 'One day, Samuel, you'll be the one to play this lyre,' he said. 'I'll teach you to play it, just like my father taught me.'

'What about me?' asked Miriam. Her mother explained that women and girls played hand-drums for when people want to dance at parties and weddings. 'I'll teach you, when you are bigger, Miriam,' she said.

Father went off to meet the other musicians. Then Samuel and Miriam and their mother set out to join the long walk to Jerusalem. There were crowds of people gathered at the bottom of the hill. 'How will we know when Father and the others are coming?' asked Miriam. 'All these people are making so much noise with their chattering.' 'Just listen carefully,' said Mother. 'You'll hear them all right.'

At first the crowd shuffled along rather slowly. Then, in the distance, they could hear a steady 'Ooo-ooo-ooo-ooo' noise from the trumpets. It got nearer and nearer. 'I can hear Father's lyre now,' said Samuel, 'and there's Uncle Zechariah's harp and Asaph's cymbals clashing away.' Soon everyone found they were keeping time, as they marched to the rhythm the musicians were playing. 'It's easy to keep in step with this steady beat,' said Miriam, 'and I do love it when all the instruments play.'

Activities

- Make home-made musical instruments. Supply a range of plastic bottles and other containers with different fillings, e.g. grit, rice, pasta, beads, etc. Plastic funnels will help.
- Bubble painting (for method see Appendix page 106).
- Blow painting (for method see Appendix page 106).

Music and rhymes

SONGS

'We all march to the beating drum' (*BBP*)

'Lord, hear our prayer' (*BBP*)

'Here come the frogs' (*BBP*) (*Make a good contrast between the verses.*)

'I love the pit, pit, patter of the rain drops' (*BBP*)

'Day oh' (*Mango Spice*)

'Mango Walk' (*Ta-ra-ra boom-de-ay*)

'Bananas in pyjamas' (*Apusskidu*)

RHYMES

'I can play on the big bass drum' (*Word Play, Finger Play*)

The rain comes pittering, pattering down,
Plipperty, plipperty, plop!
The farmer drives his horse to town,
Clipperty, clipperty clop!
The rain comes pattering,
Horse goes clattering,
Clipperty, plipperty, plop.

Speech Rhymes

Jill has a triangle,
Johnny rings a bell,
Katie shakes a tambourine,
And so does Annabelle.
James holds the cymbals,
One in each hand.
Charlie is the drummer
But I lead the band.

Zing goes the triangle,
Ring goes the bell.
Rattle bang the tambourines,
The cymbals clash as well.
Boom goes the big drum,
But my, I feel grand,
Standing on a wooden box,
A baton in my hand.

Helter Skelter

31

Drama and movement

Use a tambour to beat out different rhythms – 3/4, 4/4, 6/8, fast, slow, syncopated, etc.

Ask the children to move freely to them.

Ask children to mime different instruments for others to guess. Then all choose an instrument and mime being a band.

Another story

'I think I can hear the drum,' said Alison. 'The band must be coming. Can we open the window so we can hear it better?' she asked.

Gran came running in. She wrapped Alison in a big woollen shawl and opened the window. Yes, there it was – Boom, Boom, Boom, Boom – getting nearer and nearer. 'That's to help everyone keep in step,' Grandad explained. 'Soon we'll hear all the other instruments joining in.'

It was Gala day in the village and everyone was out in the street to watch. Except Alison. She had been poorly all week with a very sore throat and so she couldn't go out. Gran and Grandad had come to look after her because Mum and Dad were playing in the band.

'Listen,' Gran said, 'there's your dad's cornet starting up. Oh I love that tune. Too-to-too-to-to-to,' she sang. 'It comes from Wales where we used to live.'

'Now the trumpets and trombones are joining in,' said Grandad. 'And wait for it, here comes your mum on her drum.' They heard it quite clearly 'Rat-a-tat-a'. Then Alison could see all the band marching past their garden, in their smart blue and gold uniforms. 'Mum and Dad can't wave to me,' she said, 'but I'll wave to them anyway.'

They heard the sound of the music getting further and further away, but all the people in the parade who were following the band seemed to be keeping in step with the rhythm of the band.

It was so quiet when the parade had gone. Gran shut the windows and the three of them sat down for a little rest. 'I've got an idea,' said Grandad. 'Let's have our own band here.'

'But we haven't any instruments,' said Alison. 'We'll make them,' Gran decided. She fetched a big round tray from the kitchen. 'Here's the big booming drum. We'll tie a clean cloth round the end of a wooden spoon for a drumstick.' Grandad found his pocket comb and folded a tissue round it. When he blew through it, the noise was a little bit like a cornet, Gran and Alison thought.

'What can I use for a drum like Mum's?' asked Alison. She looked round the room and saw her round puzzle tin with its plastic lid, so she thought that might do. They tried it with forks, teaspoons and bigger spoons. The teaspoons were best.

When Mum and Dad came in, they were very surprised to see Grandad, Gran and Alison marching around the room. Gran was singing her favourite song 'Men of Harlech' and they were all playing their instruments in time with the tune. Of course, Mum and Dad joined in too. Afterwards they said they thought it was time for Alison to have a proper instrument of her own to play.

Which one do you think she'll choose?

Story books

- *Book of Lullabies*
- *Noisy Poems*
- *Sebastian's Trumpet*
- *Toddlerobics*

Worship time

Gather together for a quiet prayer time after a lot of noise and activity. Sing 'Lord, hear our prayer'.

NOTE

Remember that some children are frightened by too much noise.

People who help us

Aim

To help children to become more aware of the people who help them and their need to help others.

Setting
A DRESSING UP AREA

- Hats – nurse, police, traffic warden, hard hat, cook.
- Clothes – uniforms, aprons for gardening and cooking, overalls, etc.
- Objects – stethoscope, lollipop board, plastic tool box, etc.

MODEL AREA

- Play sets, e.g. road menders, ambulance, etc.

PICTURES

- Put pictures round the room, showing a wide range of people who help.

Sharing

Who has helped you today? Who helps us when we get lost, the car breaks down, we hurt ourselves, we can't find something, etc.? What can we do to help other people?

Use the setting and everything in it.

Bible story
2 KINGS 5

Sometimes Leah was very sad. She was only nine years old and she was a long way from her home and her family. She missed them very much. But in one way she was lucky; although she had to work hard in a very big house for the great lady, Hanna, Hanna was very kind to her making sure she had enough to eat and somewhere comfortable to sleep.

Sometimes in the evenings, when Leah was brushing her hair, Hanna asked Leah to tell her about her home back in Israel.

Leah told her about her mother and father in their little house in a village in the hills. 'After we'd helped in the house and looked after our animals,' she said, 'I used to play in those hills with my brothers and sisters.' She told her about going to the big town of Samaria to listen to Elisha, the clever teacher. 'He even made people better when they were ill.' That made Hanna think. She was very worried about her husband Naaman. He had a dreadful skin disease that was getting worse. Naaman was a very important man, but people wouldn't go near him because they were afraid they might catch his illness. 'Do you think this man Elisha could make Naaman better?' she asked Leah. 'I'm sure he could,' Leah replied, 'but however important Naaman is, he'll have to do exactly what Elisha tells him to.'

Hanna went straight to Naaman and told him what Leah had told her about Elisha. 'I don't know,' said Naaman. 'Elisha is a very long way away in Samaria. I don't have time to play around doing silly things.' But in the end he said he'd go, and he set off in his chariot for Samaria. Hanna and Leah had a long wait then, wondering what was happening with Elisha and Naaman.

Then one day Leah was up on the roof of the house. Suddenly she saw a cloud of dust along the road. She called to Hanna, 'I can see a chariot coming, I think it's Naaman.' They ran to meet him and what a wonderful surprise. There was a smiling Naaman, quite better from his dreadful skin disease.

'You were right, little Leah,' he said. 'Elisha asked me to do something that I thought was stupid. He asked me to bathe in a river seven times! But then I remembered what you'd said, and I decided to do exactly what Elisha told me to. I got better at once.' Then he told them that Elisha had talked to him about God and how he cares for people. 'That's what you've done for me Leah,' he said. 'You cared, Thank you.'

 ## *Activities*

- If something interesting is happening in the area (e.g. road-mending) go to see it.
- Invite a helper in to talk about what they do and to show some artefacts.
- Make a collage of people who help, using pictures from magazines.
- Make the most of the things in the setting.

 ## *Music and rhymes*

SONGS

'When I'm feeling down and sad' (*BBP*)

'We thank you God for mummies' (*BBP*) (*Add additional verses, e.g.* 'We thank you God for plumbers.')

'Jesus' hands are kind hands' (*JP*)

'Mary is a doctor' (*Knock at the Door*)

RHYMES

'Miss Polly had a dolly who was sick, sick, sick' (Traditional, from *This Little Puffin*)

'Have you been out painting?' (*Rhythm Rhymes*)

'Lollipop Lady' (*Five Furry Teddy Bears*)

'Stop! Look! and Think!' (The National Tufty Club and The Royal Society for the Prevention of Accidents, from *This Little Puffin*, 1991)

When the smoke begins to rise,
Sparks and flames shoot through the skies,
People dial 999
Then we have a go . . . So it is

One for the trousers, two for the coat,
three for the helmet, strap near my throat.
Quick, quick, hurry after me,
down the pole so slippery!

Rush to the engine; jump inside.
Hold on tight, it's quite a ride.
When we get there, day or night,
smoke and flames we have to fight.

We climb ladders towering high
and then squirt water at a house nearby.
Gradually the flames all die.
'Let's go home!' the firemen cry.

Five Furry Teddy Bears (adapted)

First of all we'll dig a hole,
fill it in, then roll, roll, roll.
Spray with tar and gravel too,
roll, roll, roll the whole day through.
Now we need some traffic signs,
kerbs and drains and long, white lines,
some Cats'-eyes which reflect the light
to help all drivers see at night.
A roundabout where four roads meet
and zebra crossing for our feet.
Then traffic lights – green, amber, red
attached to posts, and overhead.
Along the verge plant trees to grow –
the road is finished, time to go!

Five Furry Teddy Bears

I am a window cleaner
What do I do?
Climb up my ladder
And I peep at you.

I am a bus driver
What do I do?
Drive people along the road
On the 202.

I am a postie
What do I do?
Post all the letters
And here's one for you.

I am a gardener
What do I do?
I cut all the hedges
And mow the lawn too.

Finger Plays and Rhymes (adapted)

Drama and movement

Mime various activities, e.g. hanging wallpaper, controlling traffic, cleaning windows, mending cars, bandaging a cut knee, helping someone across the road, etc.

Another story

'We've got to keep our eyes open on the way home today,' said Joe, as he came out of school. 'We've been talking about people who help us and Mrs Wood has given us each different places to find out about. Mine is on the roads.' 'Right,' said Mum, 'let's start here outside school.' Sure enough, there was Gladys, stopping the traffic with her lollipop sign. Then everyone could cross safely.

Round the corner Joe caught sight of a man high up on a very tall pole. 'I wonder what he's doing up there,' said Joe. 'That looks like a dangerous job.' Mum explained that he was probably connecting up a telephone and he would be wearing a special safety harness. 'Having a telephone is going to be a good help to someone,' she said.

Further on they had to walk past a big hole in the pavement that had got red and white rails round it. There were three men, wearing bright orange helmets and fluorescent yellow waistcoats, down the hole. Then one man climbed out and Joe asked him what was happening. 'We knew there was a water leak somewhere along this road and we've just mended it,' the man said, 'so you'll still be able to have your bath tonight.'

Mum and Joe walked on. 'I can put all these people on my list of helpers,' said Joe. 'Do you think we shall see any more?' 'Well, here comes another person who helps to keep our roads safe,' said Mum. 'She's called a traffic warden, and it's her job to make sure that people park their cars in the proper places.'

Just outside their gate there was a notice that said ROAD MARKING IN PROGRESS, and there were people with a special machine painting white lines down the middle of the road and a yellow line along the side of the road. 'How does that help people?' asked Joe. 'When you grow up and learn how to drive, you'll have to learn the Highway Code,' said Mum, 'and that tells you all about where you can park your car and when you can cross over white lines.' 'The person who wrote that code was a big help too!' said Joe. 'I think my list is going to be a very long one.' Mum laughed. 'Come on into the house and I'll help you to write it out,' she said. Joe said, 'You can go on my list too!'

Story books

- *Can I Help?*
- *Jill the Farmer's Wife and Friends*
- *Let's Look at People at Work*
- *Topsy and Tim Meet the Firefighters*

Worship time

If there are enough hats, encourage the children to choose one each before gathering together for prayers. Ask them to think, first, of the sort of helper whose hat they are wearing, and, secondly, of someone who they have helped.

Tools

Aim

To help children to appreciate the skills of others and to develop simple skills of their own.

EXTRA SLOPPY WALLPAPER PASTE

BEST POTATOES

Setting

Areas for different tools, according to use:

GARDEN TOOLS

Spade, fork, trowel, rake, dibber, shears, secateurs, hose, watering can.

KITCHEN TOOLS

Whisk, wooden spoons, spatula, rolling pin, palette knife, fish slice, potato peeler, garlic press, apple corer, butter curler, melon baller, lemon squeezer, pastry cutters, slotted spoon, chapatti roller, rotary whisk, cheese grater.

DECORATING TOOLS

Paint brushes, wallpaper brushes, paste brush, rollers and tray, scraper, plumbline, pencil, expanding tape, sandpaper.

BUILDING TOOLS

Screwdriver, chisel, pliers, hammers, plane, plastering tools, adjustable wrench, g-clamp.

Sharing

Why do we need all these different things? What's the name of the box that you keep hammers and screwdrivers in? (Toolbox – all called tools.) Who uses them? What's the most useful tool you can think of for the kitchen, the garden, decorating, building?

Which tool would you use for building a wall, planting a bush, making jam tarts, etc.?

Play

Look together at the things on the tables. Decide what the tools are for. Sort them into whether the children think they are dangerous or safe. Invite a do-it-yourself expert to come in to talk about the way the tools are used.

Bible story

ISAIAH 38.12 AND 44.12–13

'I'm going to look at my dad's tools,' said Abel. 'So am I,' said his friend Saul. 'I wonder if he'll let me take one of his hammers to school to show everyone.'

The boys were having lessons at school about the different tools that people used to make all the things that are needed every day. Their teacher, Rabbi Perez, had asked them to see what tools there were in their homes and how they were used.

All this happened a long time ago, in the country where Jesus lived. There were no engines or electric machines. All the tools had to be used by hand.

Abel's father was the village weaver. He had a great big noisy loom made of wood, which was in their house. Round the walls of the room were shelves full of reels of thread in different colours. He made all the cloth for the clothes that were worn by the people of the village. Sometimes he wove wonderful patterns into the cloth. Abel said, 'I couldn't carry the loom to school, it's much too heavy. But I'll ask if I can take the piece of blue cloth Dad's just finished instead.'

'My dad has lots of different tools,' said Saul. 'A carpenter uses all sorts. He's got hammers and saws and a funny shaped thing called a plane that makes the wood really smooth. A lot of his tools have very sharp edges, he keeps them hanging up on a high shelf, but maybe a small hammer would be OK.'

Their friends Daniel and Ezra came along talking about the tools their fathers used. Daniel's father had a noisy workshop behind their house and it was often very warm in there. He needed a fire to do his work because when the metal got really hot and red and glowing, his strong arm pounded it into shape with a huge hammer. Daniel loved to watch him doing this, but he had to stand well back because of the sparks that flew about.

Just next door was the builder's yard where Ezra's father stored all the tools he needed to do his work. There were great heavy pieces of stone ready to be cut and chiselled and polished before they could be used to build houses and schools and churches. Ezra had his own little chisel and he was learning how to make marks and patterns in the stone.

The boys agreed they would go home and find out what they could take to school. Next morning they met on their way to school. Each one was carrying something from home: a hammer, a chisel, a metal bowl and Abel had the blue cloth. Daniel showed them some tools he'd found at home. They were used nearly every day. There was a wooden spoon, a big needle to sew leather and a small one for making clothes. 'Well done, all of you,' said Rabbi Perez. 'You've managed to learn a lot about tools and how important they are.'

Activities

- Cut and stick off-cuts of wallpaper on to tins and boxes.
- Use dough or clay to make simple thumb pots.
- Make biscuits using rolling pins and pastry cutters (see Appendix page 105, for recipe).
- Try card weaving (see Appendix page 105).

Music and rhymes

SONGS

'This is the way we hammer the nails', etc. (*Sing to the tune of 'Here we go round the mulberry bush.'*)

'God has given us hands' (*BBP* verse 3)

'We thank you God for mummies' (*BBP* adapted)

Use these verses:
We thank you God for builders (x3)
They build the bricks up high.

We thank you God for gardeners (x3)
They dig and plant and sow.

We thank you God for painters (x3)
They clean and rub and paint.

RHYMES

'I'd like to build a canoe for two' (*see* **Wood**, *page 27.*)

If I were not a child today,
A chef I'd like to be,
I'd chop and peel and mix and cook,
Mix and cook, mix and cook,
I'd mix and cook today.

If I were not a child today,
A carpenter I'd be,
I'd chisel, plane and hammer loud,
Hammer loud, hammer loud,
I'd hammer loud today.

If I were not a child today,
A mechanic I would be,
I'd oil and grease and fix the wheel,
Fix the wheel, fix the wheel,
Fix the wheel today.

When I grow up and I am big
I'll be a carpenter if I can
To saw, saw, saw the wood
Bang, bang, bang the nails
Oh what a lovely life.

When I grow up and I am big
I'll be a wood carver if I can
To chip, chip, chip, the wood,
Sand, sand, sand it down,
Oh what a lovely life.

Finger Plays and Rhymes (adapted)

Let us build a bungalow,
one brick on the floor.
Let us build a house now,
we need just one brick more.
Let us build some flats now,
towering to the sky,
brick on brick, brick on brick,
several storeys high.

Five Furry Teddy Bears

Drama and movement

Using big tools – building, sawing, hammering, etc. Using small tools – gardening, cooking, painting, etc.

Another story

'This is an interesting letter,' said Dad. 'It's from my sister Bridget, to say that she's coming to live near us because she has a new job.' 'What's the job?' 'When is she coming?' 'Can we go and see her soon?'

Mum and Jeremy and Ellen all asked questions together. 'One at a time,' said Dad. 'But actually I don't know the answer to your questions we'll have to ring her up.'

Bridget's new job was to work with someone who built up old motor bikes from the bits and pieces he collected from all over the place. She was starting the new job as soon as she'd found somewhere to live and she was looking forward to seeing them all soon. Jeremy and Ellen were very excited, especially about the motor bikes. A few weeks later, they all set off to see Auntie Bridget.

The workshop where she worked was down a rather muddy track. Outside the workshop, there seemed to be all sorts of things lying round – old wheels, pieces of wood, lots of tin cans and, most exciting of all, a motor bike with a funny thing like a pram beside it. 'Hello, you lot,' said a jolly voice from behind the bike. 'How do you like my new way of getting round?' There was Auntie Bridget, in her overalls, with her hair tied up in a scarf and smudges of oil on her nose and chin. The children wanted to know what she was doing and she explained she was fixing the pram thing on to the bike as a sidecar. She had a whole lot of tools laid out on a mat beside her. 'I'd know your tools anywhere Bridget,' said Dad. 'Always laid out neatly in a row.' Mum called out 'Come and look here in the workshop. They met Bob, the man Bridget worked for. He told them how his tools were always in a muddle until Bridget had arrived. Now they

hung up in neat rows, with a beautifully written notice beside each one. Just then Jeremy came in and asked for a No.6B spanner for Bridget. Sure enough there it was in the middle of the top row between 6A spanner and 6C spanner. There were still some nuts and bolts to be sorted out and the children enjoyed putting them into the right boxes on the bottom shelf.

After Bob had fetched fish and chips for them all and they'd had big tin mugs of tea (and lemonade for Jeremy and Ellen) Bridget finished off fixing the sidecar. She said the children could have a ride in it. 'We'll find some helmets to fit you and I'll take you down the drive and back. But first we must put the tools away. You can help me.'

Jeremy and Ellen couldn't stop talking all the way home – about the work they wanted to do when they grew up. Can you guess what?

Story books

- *Let's Look at Kitchens*
- *Mrs Armitage on Wheels*
- *Tales from Henry's Garden: Rumbles the Roller*

Worship time

Gather round a collection of tools from the setting. Pray for people who make things for us to use or look at. Thank God for skilled, clever people who make amazing things. Thank God for giving us brains and hands to learn how to paint and make and sew and plant.

NOTE

A good session to invite 'real craftsmen' to come and demonstrate/ join in.

Animals

Aim

To appreciate the ways in which we relate to animals and our dependency on many of them.

Pedigree for sale
please do not feed

free to a good home

sniff sniff

Preparation

Arrange in advance for a pet or pets of some kind to visit the group, along with their owner/s.

Setting

Put pictures of animals on the wall. Play a tape of animal sounds. Set up a number of areas:

VISITING ANIMALS

If possible, arrange for a pet or pets (with owners) to be present. (Take all necessary precautions! Remember *Blue Peter*!)

A FARMYARD

Use a toy set with as wide a range of animals as possible.

A PET SHOP

Gather together soft toys. Use cardboard boxes as 'cages'. Provide animal toys, leads and collars, bowls, tins of pet food, dog biscuits, etc.

A BOOK AND PICTURE CORNER

Make a collection of pictures and picture books with cushions to encourage the children to settle down and look at them.

A CRIB SCENE

Bring in the crib scene which is normally used at Christmas.

Sharing

What pets do you have? What are their names? What do they eat? Where do they sleep? What's the biggest animal you've ever seen? What's the smallest? What animals can you ride on? What animals have you ridden on?

Use the setting and everything in it. If pets have been brought in help the children to be sensitive to the way in which they are handled or approached.

Bible story
NEHEMIAH 2.12

Nehemiah was feeling very sad. His family came from Palestine, but long ago their enemies had attacked them, ruined the great city of Jerusalem and made many of the people come to live in Persia. Now there was more bad news. His brother had just arrived back from a journey to Palestine. He told Nehemiah that things were even worse than they had thought. 'There has been a great disaster in Jerusalem,' his brother said. 'The walls of the city have been flattened, all the city gates have been burnt and everything is in ruins.'

Nehemiah had an important job. He was one of the chief servants to the king of Persia. One day he was taking wine to the king and queen when the king noticed how sad he was looking. 'What is the matter, Nehemiah?' asked the king. 'Are you ill?' Nehemiah was quite frightened as he knew he ought to be cheerful with the king, but he spoke up. 'Great king,' he said, 'my city has been destroyed and no one has tried to rebuild it. Please let me go back home to work with my people to rebuild Jerusalem.' To his great surprise the king agreed. He gave him soldiers with horses to travel with him. They all set off.

When Nehemiah arrived at Jerusalem he could see that things were even worse than he had thought. The great city was a pile of rubble. For three days he stood outside the city, staring at the terrible mess. On the third night, after everyone else had gone to bed, he got up. He fetched his donkey (he knew that donkeys are very sure-footed on rough ground) and asked a few of the Persian soldiers to come with him. In the darkness they set off. They went through the Valley Gate to the Dung Gate where the big rubbish heap had been. The houses and the city walls were flattened. The great gates had been burnt. It was very difficult for the donkey, picking his way over the rubble, but Nehemiah encouraged him on. They went to the Fountain Gate and the King's Pool. After that they could not go any further. Their way was blocked by fallen stones. In the darkness they left the ruins. They went down into the valley and, by the light of the moon and stars, looked up at the city. At that moment Nehemiah knew that the time had come to begin to rebuild the city, starting with the walls.

He gathered people together to start the work. Everybody took part – farmers, builders and carpenters; an important man from the city and his daughters; caretakers, shopkeepers and makers of gold ornaments; even the High Priest. They worked hard for months and months. Nothing stopped them. As the city walls grew higher they were afraid that enemies would attack the city again so they kept weapons beside them as they built and never even stopped to get undressed.

At last the great city walls and gates were finished. They rebuilt Sheep Gate, Fish Gate, Old Gate, Valley Gate, Dung Gate, Fountain Gate, Water Gate, Horse Gate and East Gate. Nehemiah sat on his donkey, looking at the city. He remembered the day they had explored the city together. It looked very different now. Now they could start to rebuild the houses. Soon it would be a real city again.

Activities

- Make a collage of animal pictures.
- Make biscuits in animal shapes.
- Provide large sheets of paper for the children to paint pictures of the pet they have or would like to have.

Music and rhymes

Songs

'We tend our sheep' (*BBP*)

'God made furry things' (*BBP*)

'All things bright and beautiful' (Traditional)

'Rabbit ain't got no tail at all' (Apusskidu)

'I went to visit a farm one day' (Traditional, from *This Little Puffin*, 1969)

Rhymes

It's funny
my puppy
knows just how I feel.

When I'm happy
he's yappy
and squirms like an eel.

When I'm grumpy
he's slumpy
and stays at my heel.

It's funny
my puppy
knows such a great deal.

Knock at the Door

There was a young maiden called Maggie
Whose dog was enormous and shaggy;
The front of him
Looked ferocious and grim –
But the tail end was friendly and waggy.

Knock at the Door

Another story

'I think that dog of yours could learn to speak one day, Jill,' said the doctor. 'She seems to have a new trick every time I come to see you.' He bent down and tickled Goldie under her chin as she sat beside Jill. Goldie's tail thumped quietly on the floor. She seemed to know that someone was telling her how clever she was.

'I couldn't manage nearly so well without Goldie now,' said Jill, 'particularly when Bill has to go out. He knows I'll be all right with Goldie with me.'

Jill had been ill for quite a long time; she couldn't walk at all and her hands weren't very strong. She had an electric wheelchair, which had some clever tricks itself, going round tight corners and reversing into quite small spaces. When she was whizzing along the paths in the park, Jill's grandchildren said she ought to wear goggles and a helmet like a racing driver.

But in the house there were so many things that Jill couldn't do, though she and Bill had lots of gadgets to help them. That was where Goldie was such a help. She was a specially trained dog who had learned how to do things for disabled people, but she was also very clever and quickly learned new jobs. She picked up anything Jill dropped, she could carry the mobile phone to Jill in her mouth. She was very good at opening doors but not so good at closing them after her! Do you know people like that?

If Bill was out and Jill needed particular help, she could tell Goldie to press a red button by the front door and someone would come quickly.

She could even go shopping to the little shop along the road, carrying the basket with a note and some money to the shop and bringing back the paper or something that was needed. Everyone round there knew her and loved her. They knew too that Bill and Jill were the only ones to tell her what to do. Bill said that when he took Goldie for her walks, she decided where they would go.

What had surprised the doctor was seeing Goldie go into the kitchen as the washing machine stopped. She dragged the clothes basket up to the washing machine door, opened it up and pulled out the wet clothes very gently.

Just then Bill came back from town. 'What I really want to do next,' he said, 'is to teach Goldie to peg out the washing on the line.'

Everyone laughed and Goldie thumped her tail. (*This is a true story.*)

Story books

- *Animals*
- *Harry the Dirty Dog*
- *How a Zoo Works*
- *How the Zebra Got Its Stripes*
- *Let's All Dig and Burrow*

Worship time

Spend time looking at the live animal which has been brought into your group – stroking, touching, as appropriate. Talk about what the animal feels like, sounds like, smells like, how it moves. Say a prayer of thanks to God for the animal you have got to know and for all animals, which bring such variety to creation.

Going to School

Aim

To help children to feel positive and supported about new experiences such as going to school.

school

Setting

Set out in different areas:

CLASSROOM EQUIPMENT

- A low table and chairs.
- Chubby crayons, pencils, felt tips, rubbers, rulers.
- Paper of different kinds, sizes and colours.
- Exercise books, work cards, workbooks.

PRE-READING, WRITING AND MATHS

- Matching and sorting puzzles, games, etc.
- Weighing and measuring equipment.

BOOKS

- Floor cushions and low table.
- Picture books, story books, reading books, scrapbooks, picture dictionaries.

GAMES EQUIPMENT

- Balls, beanbags, skipping ropes, bats.

UNIFORM

- Uniform as used in local schools.

ACCESSORIES

- Lunch boxes, shoe bags, rucksacks, drink beakers, zipped book pockets.

Sharing

Where would you find all these things? Who goes to school? Why do we go to school? Who do you know that goes to school or college? What would you like to learn at school or college? Use the setting and everything in it.

Bible story
PROVERBS 1:7–8

'It's getting dark, Ezra,' his mother called. 'You'd better come into the house now.' Ezra and his friend Josiah had been playing a great game with some pieces of wood and a small, smooth, round stone. As the daylight faded, it was getting hard to find the stone in the grass.

'Are you getting excited about going to school tomorrow?' Josiah asked Ezra. He knew that tomorrow would be Ezra's first day. 'Yes, what's it really like?' Josiah was a bit older than he was, so he'd been going to school for a few weeks. 'It's all right,' said Josiah. 'Our teacher, Rabbi Baruch, makes us work very hard, but then he tells us wonderful stories. You'll like them.' He told Ezra that he'd come and call for him early the next morning. 'Then we can go together.' That made Ezra feel better. He ran into the house and told his mother and father that he'd have to get up early the next day to be ready to go to school with Josiah. 'That's good,' said his father. 'It's a very important day for you.'

Before settling down to sleep each night, the family said a prayer and their favourite psalm the one that begins 'The Lord is my shepherd'. 'You'll learn some new psalms at school and other things too,' Father said to Ezra. 'I still remember the psalms I learned when I was a boy. But you are luckier than I am because you've got a school in the village. There wasn't one when I was six.'

Carmel, Ezra's sister, knew she couldn't go to school, because girls didn't go in those days. But her mother taught her at home, just like her mother had taught her.

Next morning the boys set off for school together. They sat in a circle on the floor, with Rabbi Baruch. The first thing they did was to say a psalm. Rabbi Baruch began, 'The Lord is my shepherd'. Ezra sat up very tall and said it all the way through. He thought school was cool!

Activities

- Go on a walk to a local school.
- Make a packed lunch.
- Create a collage of children in the playground. (Use pre-cut outlines of children to which they can fasten material, coloured paper, etc.)

Drama and movement

Do PE activities – skipping, hopping, jumping, marching, running, creeping, catching, throwing, etc.

Music and rhymes

SONGS

'The Lord, the Lord, the Lord is my Shepherd' (*BBP*)

'Playing, running, skipping, jumping' (*BBP*)

'In our work and in our play' (*JP*)

'I jump out of bed in the morning' (*Okki Tokki Unga*) (*Make up new verses as appropriate.*)

RHYMES

What is school?
School is cool –
As a rule.

Busy,	Thinky
Happy,	Talky
Lively,	Worky
Friendly,	Playey
School	School

My best time at school
Is when we use glue,
    Sticking pictures
    Making models,
They're what I like to do.

My next best time at school
Is when I start to read,
    Story books
    Adventure books,
They're the ones I need.

My next best time at school
Is when we learn to sing
    High notes
    Low notes
I try like anything.

My next best time at school
Is when it's time to play
    In the classroom
    In the playground
We do it every day.

Another story

'Who's starting school next week then?' asked Grandad one day. 'I am, I'm nearly five,' said Jenny. 'I am, I'm going back to school,' said Mum. Jenny was very surprised. 'Are you going to my school?' she asked. 'It's for children, not grown ups.'

Mum explained that the school she was going to was called a college and it was for grown-ups. 'I'm going to learn how to be a teacher,' she said, 'so we are both going to new places, Jenny, aren't we?'

'Can I come and see your college, Mum?' Jenny asked, 'then I'll know where you are when I'm at school.' 'That's a really good idea, Jenny,' said Mum. 'Dad and I are coming with you tomorrow to see your school. My college has an Open Day on Saturday, so we can go there then.'

'Let's all go on Saturday,' said Gran. 'Perhaps your dad and grandad and I will decide to go to school too!'

Jenny had a lovely time on her school visit. She'd been there lots of times already, with her friends from playgroup. She liked Mrs Pearson, her new teacher, very much. She showed Mum and Dad where she'd keep her books and things, in a special cupboard, called a locker. It had a picture of a red balloon on the door and the same picture was by her coat hook in the cloakroom.

When he saw where Jenny could paint or play and the big, comfy cushions in the book corner Dad said that he'd like to come to school for a day. 'That would be lovely,' said Mrs Pearson. 'We like parents to come in to help. Your wife's coming in on a woodwork day.' 'I'm not much good at woodwork,' Dad said. 'I'm a chef. Could I come on a cooking day?' 'Yes please,' said Mrs Pearson and Jenny together.

On Saturday they all went to the Open Day at Mum's college. It was a huge place, much bigger than Jenny's school. Mum didn't know where her classroom would be, but she did find her locker. It hadn't got a picture on the door, just a long number that Mum said she'd have to remember. There didn't seem to be any things to play with, so Jenny was pleased it wasn't her school.

Gran was reading the notices on the big board in the hall. 'Look, there's a sewing class on Wednesday mornings,' she said. 'I'd like to do that.' 'I think I'll come at the same time, to the class about looking after cars,' said Grandad.

That just left Dad. 'Well, I've got a surprise for you. I'm coming here on Monday evenings to teach cookery at night school!' he said.

'Hooray!' said Jenny. 'We're all going to school.'

Story books

- *Anna Goes to School.*
- *At School*
- *I Don't Want To*
- *I Won't Go There Again*
- *Lucy and Tom Go to School*
- *Spot Goes to School*
- *There's a Dragon in My School*

Worship time

If you have enough children, pretend to have a short school assembly. Line up the children at the door and ask them to walk in to quiet music and sit, in rows, on the floor. Sing a song, then say prayers for friends in school, mentioning them by name.

Doors

Aim

To encourage children to explore, to discover for themselves, and to experience the excitement of finding out things.

GARAGE

49

Setting

ON THE WALLS

Put posters showing doors, if available. Put other posters and pictures on the walls. To each picture add a 'door' made from cardboard, held shut by Blue-tak.

ROUND THE DOOR/S

Decorate the door/s in some way, with streamers, balloons or pictures.

DOOR FURNITURE

On a large tray have a collection of door 'furniture' – handles, locks, keys, hinges, plaques, knockers, letter box, numbers, etc

DOOR COLLECTION

On a table put a collection of small cupboards (wooden, cardboard, cane, etc.) and/or cardboard boxes made into cupboards.

TOY DOORS

Gather together in a corner a doll's house, a garage, model cars with opening doors, Barbie's wardrobe, Action Man's tent, Duplo bricks (and people), other items with movable doors, e.g. farmyard.

Sharing

Why do we need doors? How do they open and shut? What colour is your front door? What other doors are there in your house? Which are big? Which are small? What

different kinds of doors are in your kitchen? What do you find behind doors?

Use the setting and everything in it.

Bible story

MATTHEW 1.18–2.12 AND LUKE 2.1–20

Make a large Advent calendar with sufficient doors to tell the Christmas story in sequence using pictures collected from books or old Christmas cards. Or use a book which tells the Christmas story, fastening your own doors over each picture. Save the last picture until worship time.

Activities

- Make cards with the picture inside (like opening a door).
- Use stiff white card and felt tips to make door plaques for the children's bedrooms, bathroom, etc. Provide Blu-tak for fastening them.
- Go round the building, looking at all the doors, observing the colours, knots and grain in the wood, hinges, handles, glass, keyholes, etc.
- Do some 'free' painting on large sheets of paper. Cut into door shapes, with holes cut out for windows.
- Fold paper in half. Cut window-holes in the left-hand side. Encourage children to do splatter-painting on the right-hand side. Close the door and press down. Open up to dry.

- Go for a walk in your local area. Look for doors and talk about them.

Music and rhymes

Songs

'In a cottage, in a wood' (*Okki Tokki Unga*)

'Welcome, welcome today' (*BBP*)

'Come, Lord Jesus, come' (*BBP*)

'There isn't any room' (first half of verses only) (*Carol Gaily Carol*)

Rhymes

'Knock at the door' (*This Little Puffin*)

'Here is the church' (*This Little Puffin*)

'Build a house up, build it high' (*More Word Play, Finger Play*)

I'm all made of hinges
And everything bends
From the top of my head
To the tip of my ends.
I've hinges in front
And hinges behind.
If I didn't have hinges
I couldn't unwind.

More Word Play, Finger Play

Here is the house, the roof goes so
Two little chimneys all in a row.
Clouds of smoke from the chimney go
Squiggle, squiggle, squiggle, so, so, so.
One round window, two, three, four
And right in the middle is the little green door.

Finger Plays and Rhymes

Drama and movement

Pretend to go through doors of different heights and widths. Act out opening and closing of heavy doors that need pushing and pulling, sliding doors, trap doors.

Another story

'Goodbye, Mum! goodbye, Gran!' shouted Jack as they went off for a morning's shopping trip. 'Now what are we going to do today, Grandad?' he asked. 'Doors!' said Grandad. 'That's what we're going to do today.' Jack was rather puzzled. 'How do you do doors?' Grandad explained that he had promised Gran to go round the house checking all the doors. Some of them squeaked and needed oiling, there were doors with brass handles that needed polishing and the lock on the back door was a bit loose.

By the time they sat down for their elevenses, as Grandad called their mid-morning drinks and biscuits, he had oiled all the door hinges and Jack had rubbed the brass handles until they shone. 'You've been a good help, Jack,' Grandad said. 'We'll just tighten up the screws on that lock on the back door and make sure the shed door is all right. Then we'll settle down in my den for a bit of a rest.'

Grandad's den was a little room at the back of the house. It was full of cupboards and bookshelves all loaded with books, and there was a big old desk too. Grandad settled in his comfy chair with his newspaper and Jack lay on the floor looking at some animal picture books. Soon Grandad was asleep and Jack had finished looking at books, so he wondered what to do next. I know, he said to himself, I'll check all the cupboard doors here in the den to see if they squeak. The first few doors opened easily and they didn't squeak at all. The cupboards seemed to be full of boxes of papers that didn't look very exciting, but then there was a door that was a bit stiff and Jack had to pull it quite hard. It suddenly flew open and out tumbled a pile of things with quite a clatter.

Grandad woke up with a start. He laughed when he saw what had happened. 'I've been meaning to tidy out that cupboard for ages,' he said, 'so we might as well do it now.' There were some tennis balls in a box, some golf balls in a bag and an old cap with a badge on the front and a tassel on top. 'That's from when I used to play cricket,' Grandad explained. Then, from the back of the cupboard, he brought out his cricket bat. 'I've scored some runs with this, it's a great bat,' he said. 'Maybe you'll play cricket one day, Jack, and then it'll get used again.' 'That was an exciting door to open,' said Jack, 'even if it woke you up.'

'If you promise me you won't go round opening doors that aren't yours, I'll show you an even more exciting door,' said Grandad. He unlocked the front of his big desk and pulled the top drawer right out. 'Now, watch this,' he said, and he pressed something. A little door opened at the back of the empty space. 'That's a secret door,' said Grandad. 'It opens a secret place where Gran and I keep some special papers. Your mum knows about it and now you do too.' When Mum and Gran came home Jack told them he liked doing doors, especially secret ones.

Story books
- *The Aircraft*
- *Alfie Gets in First*
- *Big Book of Noah's Ark*
- *This Is the Star*

Worship time
Gather around the Advent calendar. Open the last door and talk about it. Sing either 'Come, Lord Jesus, come' or 'There isn't any room'.

NOTE

This theme is particularly suitable for use during Advent, though it would be possible to substitute another story for the Bible story.

Greetings

Aim

To help children realize the importance of making people welcome.

53

Setting

Try to make the room particularly welcoming with a rug, floor cushions, a table with flowers, pictures, banners and posters round the walls and a welcoming person. On low tables place nibbles (not nuts), drinks, a telephone and greeting cards of different kinds.

Welcome children as they come in and let them play with the setting.

Sharing

What do you say to people who you meet or who come to visit? What does your face do then? Do you know what people in any other countries say when they meet each other? (E.g. Bon jour (France), Guten Tag (Germany), Buenos dias (Spain), Shalom (Israel), Jambo (Kenya).

Can you think of times when you send special cards to people? (Christmas, birthday and new home, new job, driving test, etc.) What special cards do you have sent to you?

Bible story

LUKE 2.8–10

'Where's our Jacob? Late as usual, I suppose,' said Reuben. 'It's time we were off up on those hills. The sheep will be wondering where we've got to.'

Reuben, Micah and Joel were shepherds, who looked after a big flock of sheep at night, when they'd all been gathered together. They knew Amos and Daniel would be waiting for them to take over guard duty after their long day out on the hills. During the day the sheep and their lambs wandered around looking for fresh sweet-tasting grass to eat. At night they usually huddled together to keep warm, so it was not difficult to look after them, but then there was always the danger of wild animals who liked a tasty bit of sheep for supper.

'Hello there,' came a voice from the dark village street, 'Sorry to keep you all waiting,

I'd forgotten to fill up my lamp with oil.' It was Jacob at last, hurrying along carrying his lamp, his warm cloak and his good thick stick. They all had these, in case they had to fight off a wolf or a lion.

Reuben whistled for Zac their dog to follow them and off they all went. As they got near to the top of the hill they could see the glow of a fire and the lights of two lamps belonging to Amos and Daniel. They were waiting to go home. 'We're really glad to see you,' was their greeting. 'It's pretty cold up here and we want to get to our homes and warm beds.' There was the soft noise of breathing from the sleeping sheep and the sound of one or two tails thumping on the ground. 'There you are. We knew you'd be pleased to see us,' said Joel.

Soon the shepherds were settled round the fire, with their warm cloaks wrapped round them. 'There's something different about tonight,' said Micah. 'Even the stars seem brighter, and just look at that brilliant one over Bethlehem. Isn't it still and quiet?'

It was certainly very, very quiet and they all drew closer to each other. It seemed as though something mysterious was going to happen. Then suddenly the whole sky seemed full of a bright light. It was so bright that their eyes were dazzled and they could feel their hearts bumping away. A marvellous clear voice seemed to come out of the light. 'Don't be afraid,' it said. 'I've come to tell you something wonderful. A baby is being born tonight in Bethlehem. He is the very best person ever to be born and he will be the most important person ever to live in this world.' The shepherds looked at each other. They weren't afraid at all, just surprised. Lovely music seemed to be all round them, even the sheep and Zac the sheepdog had sat up. 'Look, they are listening too,' whispered Jacob. 'Isn't it the most beautiful thing you've ever heard?'

When it was all quiet and still again, the shepherds decided they wanted to go and see this baby. 'We can't all go and leave the sheep,' said Reuben. 'Micah, you and Jacob go first and Joel and I will go when you get back.' 'That's fine,' said Micah, 'and we'll take a lamb as a present but, just a minute, what do you say to an important baby, is he like a king?' Nobody really knew.

When they got to the place in Bethlehem, and knocked on the door, voices said 'Please come in. We are glad that you have come.' There was the baby Jesus fast asleep with Joseph and Mary looking so happy and pleased to see them. 'Hello Jesus,' said Micah and Jacob. 'You are very welcome in our world.'

Activities

- Make greeting cards using collage, paint, felt pens, etc.
- Invite some visitors and prepare drinks and nibbles for them.
- Give the children circles on which to draw smiley faces. Thread them on to string to make a 'smiley face' garland.

Music and rhymes

Songs

'Welcome, welcome today' (*BBP*)

'Let today be the day' (*BBP*)

'We tend our sheep' (*BBP*)

'Oh, who would be a shepherd boy' (*Carol, Gaily Carol*)

'It's birthday time for . . .' (*BBP*)

'The Peace of the Lord be always with you' (*BBP*)

'Good day, good day to you, Good day, oh dipidu' (*Tinderbox*)

'Happy birthday to you' (*as appropriate*)

'We wish you a merry Christmas' (*Carol, Gaily Carol*)

Rhymes

Writing letters, writing letters,
pencil in my hand.
Scribble, scribble, scribble,
I hope you'll understand.

Drawing pictures, drawing pictures,
colours red, green, blue.
Squiggles, circles, splodges
especially for you.

Posting letters, posting letters,
envelopes in hand.
Each one with a stamp on
to travel over land.

Five Furry Teddy Bears

Drama and movement

Use different sorts of welcome:

- Shake hands with one hand.
- Shake hands with two hands.
- Right hands flat clap in the air.
- Rub noses.
- Hug.
- Kiss on both cheeks.
- Hands together and bow.
- Curtsey.

Another story

'We've got something very special to do today,' Mrs Bevan told the children at playgroup. 'Some important visitors are coming to see us tomorrow and we've got to think of how to welcome them. Has anyone got any ideas?'

'My grandma's got a mat by the door to her flat that says welcome in big yellow letters. Can we do that?' said Carol. 'Mats take rather a long time to make,' said Mrs Bevan, 'Maybe we could do a big notice, like a banner, to hang over the door.'

'Can we tie some balloons on the gate?' Keith asked. 'We do that when we have a party at our house.' 'That's a good idea,' said

Mrs Russell. We can paint smiley faces on them too.'

Very soon the children were busy, all covered up with old shirts as aprons. Mrs Bevan got out an old sheet and they painted it in bright colours. Mrs Russell found some black paper and cut out the letters to make WELCOME. Then some children stuck shiny paper shapes and sequins on the letters. When the banner was all put together it looked really good. 'If we hang it up near a light,' said Mrs Russell, 'those shiny bits will twinkle like stars.'

At singing time, the children practised their favourite songs, so they would be able to sing some of them to their visitor. They even made up a new one, to the tune of 'Happy Birthday to you'. It went like this:

Warm welcome to you,
Warm welcome to you,
Warm welcome to our visitors,
We're glad to see you.

Then the children drew smiley faces on the balloons with felt pens. It wasn't very easy because they didn't want the balloons to go pop.

Instead of Playdough that day, they had real dough to roll out and cut into star shapes, to be baked as biscuits for their visitors. When they were cooked the children spread pink icing on each one and decorated them with little sweets. 'Will there be some of these biscuits for us too?' asked Peter. 'They look lovely.' 'Oh yes,' said Mrs Russell. 'We'll all have a party together, with juice for you and coffee and tea for our visitors.'

'Who are these visitors?' asked one of the children. 'Do you think they'll like all the things we've done for them?' 'It's the mayor and mayoress of our town, who are coming,' explained Mrs Bevan. 'They'll probably come in a big black car and they'll be wearing lovely gold chains. They want to come and see what we do at our playgroup.'

Next day the children were quite excited to see their balloons tied on the gate in big bunches. Then just over the door was the big

welcome banner they had made, with the shiny paper and sequins twinkling.

The visitors came right on time, in their big gleaming black car. They laughed at the happy faces on the balloons and said they felt very welcome when they saw the banner that the children had made over the door. In fact they enjoyed everything, watching the children with the sand and water and drawing pictures with them. The mayoress said that she hadn't remembered to bring her apron, so she'd better not do any painting. The mayor had two iced biscuits with his coffee, he said they were so good. There were enough for everyone else to have one as well.

After the children had had a good look at the beautiful gold chains the mayor and mayoress were wearing, they sang some songs to them. 'That welcome song you children made up for us is super,' said the mayor. 'We've had a lovely time. Thank you very much for helping us to enjoy our visit.'

Story books
- *Alfie Gives a Hand*
- *Hello Goodbye*
- *The Jolly Postman*
- *Letters*
- *The Surprise Party*

Worship time
Gather in the setting around the welcome table. Sing 'The Peace of the Lord be always with you' and then shake hands with everyone else.

Rough and smooth

Aim

To help children to realize the importance of different textures which make God's world more functional and interesting.

Setting

Arrange the materials in four different areas around the room.

HARD THINGS

- Pebbles and stones.
- Bricks and rocks.
- Rough and smooth sea shells.
- Coral.
- Planed and unplaned wood, bark.
- Smooth and rough metal.
- Wicker baskets.

SOFT THINGS

- Tweed, silk, satin, velvet, hessian, felt.
- Different types of hand knitting.
- Crochet and lace.
- Bubble plastic.

PAPER PRODUCTS

- Paper, card, sandpaper, tissue paper, crêpe paper.
- Greaseproof paper, waxed paper, parchment, rice paper.
- Foil paper, corrugated card, vyvelle (if available).
- Home made paper, newspaper, toilet paper, tissues.
- Wallpaper, textured and plain.
- Blotting paper, computer paper.

GROWING THINGS

- Holly, ivy, cactus.
- Flowers and leaves.
- Conifers, pampas, bulrushes, teasels.
- Variety of vegetables including cabbage, onion, potatoes, cauliflower, sweetcorn (some cut in half).
- Variety of fruit including pineapple.

Sharing

How do you know whether something is rough or smooth? Shut your eyes and think of something smooth. What are you thinking about? Shut your eyes and think of something rough. What are you thinking about?

Use the setting to sort each area into rough and smooth.

Bible story
LUKE 3.5

'Hey, come here and look, Josiah,' shouted his friend Abner. 'There's a great cloud of dust coming along the road; I wonder what it is.'

The boys often played by the big main road that went near their house. They liked to watch the people who came past. There were no cars or lorries like we see on our roads – not even any motor bikes or bicycles. Nearly everyone walked. Sometimes there were donkeys with big bundles on their backs. Once or twice they had seen camels; that was very exciting.

The road wasn't much like our roads either. It was rough and stony and when it rained hard, everyone had to pick their way through thick brown mud. But mostly it was like today, very dusty. Josiah and Abner watched carefully. 'It's a lot of dust,' they said to each other. 'There must be a lot of people coming.' Then they could hear a noise – tramp, tramp, tramp, tramp – a regular rhythm. 'I know what that is,' said Abner. 'It's soldiers marching in step, I wonder where they are going.'

Josiah was a bit frightened. 'Let's hide behind this rock,' he said. 'We can see them and they won't notice us.'

As they peeped over the rock, they heard the leading soldier shout 'Halt!' and the marching stopped. 'This is a good place to work out where our new road is to go.' Soon the soldiers were busy measuring the ground with long sticks and putting little pieces of wood into the ground to show where the road should go. Some of them dug holes as well.

'We have to find out what's under all these rough stones if we are going to build the road here,' said the centurion – he was the leader. 'I know it gets very muddy on this bit when it rains hard.' He seemed pleased, so he got the soldiers lined up again. 'Quick march!' he ordered and off they went. The cloud of dust made by their feet got smaller and smaller and the tramping noise died away.

Josiah and Abner came out from their hiding place to look at what the soldiers had done. 'I think it's going to be a very straight road,' said Abner. 'Let's come again to see how they build it.' So the boys kept coming back. Each time something different had happened. At first, the stones from the old road were dug up and piled at the sides and the space was filled with mud that had set really hard. Next these stones were put back on top of the mud, mixed up with bits of broken cups and plates.

Then one day they found there were great big flat stones fitting together like a jigsaw puzzle, on top of everything. The boys loved to run along this smooth surface. 'No clouds of dust now,' said Josiah. 'And no sticky mud either,' agreed Abner.

Days later John the Baptist was on his way to baptize people in the River Jordan. He walked along the brand new road. It was gentle to his feet after all the rough roads he usually walked on. He remembered the words of the Bible, 'winding paths shall be made straight and rough places smooth'. He knew that when Jesus came he would make life better for people, just as the soldiers had turned a rough path into a smooth road.

Activities

- Put different objects into small bags or socks, fastened with rubber bands. Ask the children to feel them and guess what they are.
- Do fruit and vegetable prints on various kinds of paper.
- Make a collage with different sorts of fabric and paper.
- Make a garden on a tray.

- Use the sides of wax crayons or chalk to do rubbings of different textures.

Music and rhymes

SONGS

'Caring, sharing' (*BBP*)

Use this new verse:

Touching (touching) Feeling (feeling)

Stroking (stroking) Rubbing (rubbing)

'She'll be coming round the mountain when she comes' (*Apusskidu*)

Use the following verses and make up some of your own:

She'll be riding on the doormat when she comes . . .

She'll be wearing silk pyjamas when she comes . . .

She'll be eating crispy cabbage when she comes . . .

She'll be slipping on the shingle when she comes . . .

She'll be popping bubble plastic when she comes . . .

RHYMES

Today as I went out to play

I saw a brown frog in the way.

I know that frogs are smooth and green,

But this was brown – what could it mean?

I asked a lady in the road;

She said it was a spotted toad!

Knock at the Door

Drama and movement

Mime a range of activities which involve rough and smooth textures, e.g.

Stroking a cat.

Brushing a dog.

Scrubbing an elephant.

Digging the garden.

Sliding across ice.

Another story

'I do hope we have some snow soon,' said Jean one night, when she was going to bed. 'There wasn't more than a sprinkling of snow last year.' Dad had just come home from work and he heard her. 'It's fun for you children and people who like sledging and ski-ing,' he said. 'But it can make going anywhere quite difficult and sometimes it's dangerous too.'

Then Mum told them she'd just heard the weather forecast on the radio, and it seemed as if it might snow that night. Just then they noticed a lorry passing their house with a yellow light flashing on its roof. There seemed to be a rattling noise at the same time. 'What's that?' asked little Sam. 'Ah, that's the grit lorry,' said Dad. 'It's spreading tiny little stones and salt on the road to make it a bit rough, so cars won't slip if the road gets smooth and icy.' 'Will it spoil the snow?' Jean asked anxiously. 'I want everywhere to look white.' 'Don't worry,' said Mum. 'If it snows a lot there'll be plenty to cover everything.'

Next morning, as soon as the children woke up, they knew it had snowed in the night because the bedroom seemed full of whiteness. They pulled back the curtains, and there was a beautiful white world. Soft feathery snowflakes were dancing past the window. There were a few cars going along the road, very slowly and carefully. 'It's a good thing there was grit there,' said Dad as he came into their bedroom, 'or they'd never be able to get anywhere.'

As soon as breakfast was over, Jean and Sam wanted to go out. 'I'll wear my brown shoes,' said Jean. 'They've got really smooth bottoms, so I can slide well.' 'That's not a good idea,' said Mum. 'Your feet will quickly get wet and cold and slides are dangerous.' She told them that when she was a girl, she'd walked out of her gate on to the pavement one snowy day. Some children had made a smooth slide and her feet slipped on the snow. Next minute she was whizzing down the hill on her bottom, ending up in a hedge on the corner. 'I wasn't hurt,' she said, 'but it was dangerous, an old person could have fallen and broken an arm or leg. You two put on thick socks and your wellies and we'll all go and find a safe sliding place in the park.'

Soon they were on their way. The snow was quite deep, it nearly came to the top of Sam's wellies. Dad had cleared their path with a big snow shovel, and he'd fetched some grit from the box on their road and spread it, so that the ground was rough. Mum had a funny looking parcel under her arm. 'What's that for?' asked Sam. 'Wait and see,' said Mum.

In the park, they rolled snow into a big smooth ball. They made a smaller one and put it on top. Dad had some rough stones and a carrot in his pocket and they gave the snowman eyes and a nose.

Mum's parcel turned out to be the thick plastic bag that had had logs for the fire in it. It was brilliant. They all took turns sitting on it and whoosh! They were off down the hill. Sam sat in front of Mum and she held him tight. Jean went with her dad and then managed one go on her own. By the time they got home, they all had smooth, rosy cheeks, very cold fingers and toes and they were so hungry. 'What a lovely time we've had. I'm so glad it snowed,' said Jean.

Story books
- *My First Look at Touch*
- *Spot's Touch and Feel Book*
- *Touch*
- *Touch and Feel Wild Animals*

Worship time
Ask everyone to hold something from the setting. Sing the new verse to the tune of 'Caring, sharing' (*BBP*).

Seaside

Aim

To help children to discover that the seaside is not just about fun, but is an important element in the lives of many people.

fishing nets, rods and a packet of fish fingers. Beside this, on the floor, place a plastic sheet underneath a water bath with plastic ships and fish.

Preparation

To keep the floor clean and to make it easier to clean up the sand, put an old shower curtain or waterproof sheet underneath the various settings.

 ## Setting

IN THE CENTRE

Lay down a length of sand-coloured fabric and a piece of blue fabric on top of the waterproof material.

ON THE SAND-COLOURED FABRIC

Scatter sand and add shells, driftwood, pebbles, fishing net and any other natural artefacts found on the beach.

ON THE BLUE FABRIC

Place an inflated boat which is big enough for a child to sit in.

IN A CORNER OR AT THE SIDE OF THE ROOM

Place fabric or a towel with a seaside design. On it put buckets and spades, swimming costumes and other seaside gear.

ON A SIDE TABLE

Put a blue cloth, then place ships, Lego for dock building, paper or papier mâché fish,

 # Sharing

When I say seaside what do you think of? What do you enjoy doing with sand? What do you enjoy doing in the water? What do we see in the sea? What do we see on the sea? What kinds of different boats are there? What do people do on boats?

In the setting encourage the children to take off their shoes and play 'seasides': row the boat; play with the seaside area.

 # Bible story
MATTHEW 4.18–22

He stood and watched them for a long time. Two men were standing in the lake and the water was up to their waists. They were quite a way apart from each other and they appeared to be holding something. Then they began to walk towards the shore and he could see that they were holding a long fishing net. As they got nearer he could see there were silver things jumping up and down in the water as if they were trying to get away. Jesus realized that they were fish.

He watched the men come in and sort the fish. They kept the good ones and the small ones were thrown back into the water to grow bigger.

Jesus walked down on to the shore and chatted to them about their fishing. They told him that some days there were lots of fish and other days there were very few. It all depended on the weather and the winds. Fish go really deep in the water some days.

Jesus discovered that the two men were brothers and that they were called Simon and Andrew. They asked who he was and he explained that he was a sort of fisherman too. He was catching people. They didn't understand but when he asked them if they would help him with his task, they said, 'Yes, it sounds interesting,' and they left their fishing and went with him.

A little further along the lake shore he saw three more men sitting in a boat which they had pulled out on to the dry land. There were two young men and an older man. Jesus soon discovered that the older man was their father and his name was Zebedee.

They were using a special piece of wood and some sisal to mend the holes in the fishing nets. They explained to Jesus how the nets got broken. It was sometimes the big fish that were very heavy, but it was usually because the nets got caught on old tree branches and rubbish while they were pulling them through the water.

Jesus talked for a long time with Zebedee. He had been fishing all his life and had lots of fishy stories to tell. Jesus asked the sons, James and John, if they would like to join him and help with his work. They thought it would be an adventure. So they decided to follow Jesus.

Activities

- Sand painting: Use a mixture of paint and paste, large brushes and sugar paper or cereal pack card. When the children have completed the painting let them sieve or sift sand over it, shaking off the excess.
- Pebble collages: Stick pebbles on to cereal packet card cut into shapes, or polystyrene trays, using Children's Glue.

- Junk boats: Build boats from junk.
- Pebble painting: Paint the pebbles with a mixture of PVA glue and paint using small brushes.

Music and rhymes

SONGS

'Row, row, row your boat' (*Knock at the Door*)

'One day when we were fishing' (*BBP*)

'Jesus called to Peter the fisherman' (*BBP*)

'Jesus went a-walking by the seashore' (*Story Song*)

'Fishing, fishing, down by the sea' (*Okki Tokki Unga*)

'Sons of the sea' (*Okki Tokki Unga*)

RHYMES

Five little children
Walking on the shore
One stopped to catch a crab
And then there were four.

Four little children
Walking by the sea
One saw a jelly fish
And then there were three.

Three little children
Said, 'What can we do?'
One threw a great big stone
And then there were two.

Two little children
Having lots of fun
One got his clothes wet
And then there was one.

One little sad girl
Alone by the sea
Found all her friends again
And went home for tea.

Look behind you!
Look behind you!
Patterns on the beach
Running footsteps,
Walking footsteps,
All within your reach.
Wiggles with your fingers,
squiggles with your toes –
as the tide comes in and out
all the pattern goes.

Look behind you!
Look behind you!
Patterns in the sand.
There are big marks
and little marks
made by foot or hand.
Faces with your fingers,
letters with your toes –
as the tide comes in and out
all the pattern goes.

Five Furry Teddy Bears

Drama and movement

Act out: Splashing steps; Putting toes into cold water; Swimming on the carpet; Jumping over the waves; Putting up the sail; Hauling in the fishing boats.

Another story

This story works well if done actively with the children, using their ideas and suggestions.

OUTLINE OF STORY

Everyone asleep – alarm clock goes off.

Lovely day for trip to seaside, what to wear?

Getting ready: finding buckets, etc., folding towels, making sandwiches, pack a bag.

How to get there? Coach, train, car.

What to do first? Settle on sands, wriggle into swimsuits, rub on sun cream, insist on hats!

Let's try water: dip in toe, paddle, splash, swim.

Dry on large towel, run to keep warm.

Search in rock pools for shells, pebbles, sea creatures.

Picnic, dealing with litter.

Games with balls, bats, drawing on sand, kite-flying.

Buying ice cream, candyfloss, chips.

Donkey rides, rowing, climbing rocks.

Time to pack up – run for coach, train.

Going home – singing.

Off to sleep. Thank you for a lovely day!

Story books
- *A Day Out*
- *The Lighthouse Keeper's Catastrophe*
- *Lucy and Tom at the Seaside*
- *Magic Beach*
- *The Smallest Whale*
- *The Whale's Story*

Worship time

Ask each child to pick a stone or shell and to sit round the seaside setting. Listen to a tape of waves breaking on the shore. Say prayers of thanks for the beauty of the seaside, the things that are found there, the fun that can be had there and the people who live and work there.

Holes

Aim

To help children to discover that even simple things like holes are exciting.

Setting

Areas in room.

NATURAL OBJECTS WITH HOLES

- Wood, stone, clay, bark, leaves, fruit and vegetables, coral, fossils, bowls of bulb fibre with holes for planting bulbs.

MANUFACTURED OBJECTS

- Sieves, colanders, teapots, candlesticks, decorative china, pasta, large beads.
- Lace, broderie anglaise, sequin strips, buttons.
- Doilies, doughnuts, biscuits, sweets (Polos).
- Posting boxes.
- Hoops, child's tunnel, shapes into holes games, cribbage board.
- Trellis, bird feeders, flowerpots.

HOLES THAT NEED MENDING

- Socks, tights, jeans, elbows of sweaters.
- Pictures of road-mending, Playmobil® construction team sets.

WHERE CREATURES LIVE

- Nesting box, pictures of holes for birds, insects and animals, wasps' nest, honeycomb.

Sharing

Where can we find a hole? Think of a really big hole and a tiny one. What's a really useful hole? Who could use it? What's a hole that is a nuisance? What can we do about holes like that? Use the setting and everything in it to explore holes.

Bible story

MATTHEW 8.20

'It's getting very hot, Jesus,' said Peter. 'Let's stop and rest under those shady almond trees, just up there along the road.' 'Yes,' said Andrew. 'There's a little stream, so we can have cool water to drink with our lunch.' James said, 'Look, there are some fig trees too – we can have fresh fruit to finish off the meal. It's an ideal spot for our picnic.'

Jesus and his friends were walking from the village of Yif'af over the hills to Gevat. They had started out early in the morning when it was cool, but now they were ready to rest. They all settled down under the welcome shade of the trees beside the road. There were low smooth rocks to sit on, and bigger ones to lean against while they ate their meal. It was so quiet and peaceful, no one wanted to move on. Little insects and lizards scuttled past and they could hear birds up in the trees above their heads.

Then John whispered to the others, 'Just look at that! Keep quiet everyone!' They watched, not making a sound, as a fox's head came out of a hole between some rocks across the road. It seemed as if the fox was checking whether it was safe to come right out. All was quiet and still, so the men watched and waited to see what would happen next.

The fox came right out of the hole, sniffing the air carefully. She must have felt it was safe, because three little foxes, her young cubs, popped out of the hole. They seemed to be ready for fun because they ran and jumped and rolled over each other, while mother fox watched them proudly. She barked at them if they wandered too far off from her. A game of hide and seek started, with each little fox cub hiding and then jumping out on the others. Then one of them tumbled head over heels out of the tuft of grass where he'd been hiding. Jesus and the others watching the fox family couldn't help laughing out loud. Quick as a flash, mother fox barked once and she and the cubs disappeared down the hole.

'That was fun,' said Peter. 'I'm so glad we saw them playing like that. Didn't they go quickly when they realized we were around?'

Jesus sighed and said, 'They have a warm safe home down in that hole, where the young foxes can grow up. We can't do what God wants and at the same time stay in our safe homes.' 'No,' said Andrew, 'but we still want to be with you.'

Activities

- Use Playdoh or similar with a garlic press.
- Make rings from Newclay to hold candles.
- Visit a road-mending site.
- Plant bulbs in holes in flower pots or gardens.
- Use wool and bodkins to make items from plastic canvas (7 holes to 2 $\frac{1}{2}$ cm).
- Use doilies as stencils to paint over and produce patterns.
- Put a cloth or blanket over a table so that the children have a 'hidey-hole' in which to play.
- Play hide and seek.

Music and rhymes

SONGS

'There's a hole in my bucket' (*Apusskidu*)

'God has put a circle round us' (*BBP*)

RHYMES

'A little mouse lived in a hole' (*Finger Plays and Rhymes*)

First of all we'll dig a hole,
fill it in, then roll, roll, roll.
Spray with tar and gravel too,
roll, roll, roll the whole day through.

Five Furry Teddy Bears

When children are asleep in bed
(*Curl up on the floor.*)
and darkness fills the sky,
the creatures of the night wake up,
(*Slowly uncurl, yawn and stretch.*)
as Mr Owl flies by.
(*Tu-whit, tu-whoo*)

They stop, they wait till he has gone,
then rabbits, mice and voles
(*Sit up and point to each other.*)
creep out beneath the moon and stars
from burrows and from holes.
(*Proceed carefully from holes on all fours.*)

They rush about to find some food,
(*Crawl quickly about.*)
then eat, then rest or play.
(*Smile and dance.*)
But when they hear tu-whit, tu-whoo,
(*Make owl sounds.*)
they quickly run away!
(*Children run to safety.*)

Five Furry Teddy Bears

Drama and movement

Explore holes of different sizes using minute and large movements. Crawl through holes, pop out of holes, feel the way in the dark as if in a tunnel.

Use the rhyme 'When children are asleep in bed' (see above) for drama and movement.

Another story

'The rain's stopped,' said Gran. 'Let's put on our wellies and go for a walk.' Josh and Pauline were spending the day at her house and they'd been indoors all morning because of the wet weather.

'Where can we go?' asked Josh. 'I really wanted to play football in the park, but the grass will be too wet and soggy, won't it?'

'I'm afraid so,' said Gran. 'But I've got a special "find a hole" walk for you, so come on.'

The children thought this was a bit funny, but off they went.

As soon as Gran had shut the front door, she showed them the first holes – the keyhole and the letter-box. Then there was one in the gate-post, where the catch fitted in. 'You'll have to keep your eyes wide open to find holes on this walk,' said Gran. 'Let's see what you can see.'

Pauline spotted the next hole. It was the drain, where the water in the gutter, like a little stream, was rushing down. It was a very useful hole because after heavy rain there could be floods. Round the corner Josh was really interested in a big yellow digger. The workmen with it were mending a hole in the road. They stopped to watch for a bit. 'I'm glad that hole is being filled in,' said Gran. 'My car used to bump when it went over it.'

They went through a gate on to a path at the side of a field. Gran showed them some holes in the field quite near the path. 'Those are rabbit holes,' she said. 'Sometimes I walk along here in the evening and keep very quiet and I've seen the rabbits popping in and out.'

'Who lives in that hole?' asked Pauline pointing to one at the bottom of a big tree. 'Do you think it could be a bear?' She looked rather worried.

'No,' said Gran. 'I'm not exactly sure, but I expect it's a very small animal like a weasel.' She pointed to a hole quite high up in another tree. 'That could belong to a squirrel or maybe even a woodpecker. It makes holes like that with its strong sharp beak.'

The path went down to a little stream and the children looked round for more holes.

Josh went so near the edge of the stream that he nearly slipped in. 'Come back, Josh!' Gran called. 'It would make a big hole in the water if you fell in!' 'I can see some holes in that bank across the stream,' said Josh. 'I think water rats live there – I've read about them in my *Wind in the Willows* book.' 'Well done, Josh,' said Gran. 'They are not easy to spot.'

Then Pauline found some even smaller holes, tiny little round ones in the wooden rail of the bridge over the stream. They all looked very carefully and decided it was where nails had been hammered in and later pulled out. Gran explained that sometimes little holes like that were made by woodworms which ate the wood.

The very last hole on the walk was a good one. Gran had some little minty sweets with holes in the middle which they all enjoyed. 'When we get to our house,' said Josh, 'I'm going to ask if we can go for a "ind a hole" walk. It's great!'

Story books

- *Holes and Peeks*
- *Mole in a Hole*
- *Owl Babies*
- *Who's in Holes?*

Worship time

Either gather closely together into a circle made by rope or into a number of circles provided by hoops. Pray together, remembering that, wherever we are, we are in God's care. Sing together 'God has put a circle round us' (*BBP* – verses 1 and 3).

Weddings

Good Luck

Preparation

Send a note home the previous week asking children to bring in wedding photographs of people they know.

 # Setting

In different areas of the room display the following:

HEADGEAR

- Male: top hats, uniform caps, tam-o'-shanter, yarmulke (Jewish skull cap), turban, African 'pillbox', etc.
- Female: large, flowery headdresses, veils, flower bands, tiaras, etc.

OUTFITS

- Male: tail coats, pinstripe trousers, jackets, waistcoats, bow ties, cravats, kilts, polished shoes.
- Female: bridesmaids' dresses, party dresses, wedding dresses, wedding shoes.
- Accessories: garter, horseshoe, bags, button-holes, bouquets, gloves.

OTHER ITEMS

- Photographs, albums, wedding cake in boxes, invitations, order of service, place cards, balloons, ribbon, camera, wrapped presents, rings.

 # Sharing

Play some music used at weddings, e.g. the Bridal March (Lohengrin), Vidor's Toccata and Fugue. Ask the children where they might have heard the music. What does it remind them of? Invite them to talk about weddings they have been to.

Encourage the children to explore the setting and everything in it.

Bible story
MATTHEW 25.1–13

'Now, have you all made sure your lamps have got enough oil for the wedding procession tonight?' said Tabitha to her sisters. 'Everyone expects you bridesmaids to lead the way to the bridegroom's house.' The girls were getting ready for Tabitha's wedding. They helped her dress in her best clothes and put on the beautiful jewellery that Benjamin, the bridegroom, had given her. 'You look so lovely,' said little Abigail. 'I have to keep remembering you are still my big sister.'

Hannah was a bit worried. 'There aren't many of us to light the way,' she said. 'I hope there will be more bridesmaids with lamps joining us.' 'Yes,' said Dorcas, 'and that they'll remember to put enough oil in their lamps too.'

As it began to get dark, the bride's procession was ready to walk through the streets to Benjamin's house. They knew he would send them a signal when he was ready to come and meet them with his procession. Then they would all go to the feast in his home.

Tabitha's sisters, who were the bridesmaids, lit their lamps, ready to lead the way. Her aunts and girl cousins got out their hand drums and bells, and they all waited and waited. 'I hope this gives the other bridesmaids time to join us with their lamps,' Hannah said anxiously. 'Where can they be?'

Just then a message came to say everything was ready. 'I think those bridesmaids must have forgotten to fill their lamps with oil,' said Tabitha's father.

People came out of their houses to watch the procession go past. It was a wonderful sight. Everyone was singing and dancing and the lamp flames flickered and lit up the happy faces.

It was such a lovely wedding and they all enjoyed eating the food at the feast. Benjamin and Tabitha were a very handsome couple and Tabitha's sisters were excellent brides-maids.

'Well done, girls,' she said to them. 'What a good thing you checked the oil in your lamps.'

Activities

- Provide large shapes (bells, hearts, horseshoes, etc.). Decorate them to make a wedding collage using traditional confetti and rose petals.
- Provide net curtains, long lacy petticoats, headdresses, shoes, bags, bow ties, waistcoats, top hats for a dressing up activity.
- Use fresh, dried or silk flowers to make bouquets, buttonholes and table decorations or to decorate straw hats.

Music and rhymes

SONGS

'Welcome, welcome today' (*BBP*)

'Give me oil in my lamp, keep me burning' (*CP*)

'Come and join the celebration' (*H&P*) (*Change last line to 'There's a wedding on today'*)

If you're happy and you know it, clap your hands, (*clap, clap*) x 2

If you're happy and you know it, then you surely want to show it,

If you're happy and you know it clap your hands.

If you're happy and you know it, ring the bell, etc.

If you're happy and you know it cut the cake, etc.

If you're happy and you know it dance around, etc.

If you're happy and you know it have a hug, etc.

Traditional

RHYMES

The car's being polished,
Our shoes are polished too.
I really wonder why,
What are we going to do?

Look at my new suit,
And mum's flowery hat,
And dad's bright blue waistcoat,
What do you think of that?

At last they say we're ready,
Off to church we'll go.
It's Aunty Mary's wedding,
She's marrying Uncle Joe.

Drama and movement

Mime a wedding procession going down the aisle. Use a tape of suitable music.

Play a tape of bell-ringing and do the actions to go with it.

Sing and dance the Hokey Cokey or dance to suitable pop music.

Another story

'What shall I wear?' Margaret had been invited to a very special wedding. She wanted to look very nice. She decided to go to town to look for a special hat. What colour should it be? she thought. There were so many to choose from. Big ones, feathery ones, small ones, ones with roses, ones with bows, ones with big brims and ones with small brims. Some hats were tall, some were wide and some were made like little caps with great big feathers.

Margaret tried on so many and at last she decided on a large cream hat with a wide brim and a big bow as it would go very well with her new blue dress. The lady at the shop said that as it was a large hat she needed a hat box for it. So Margaret paid and went home carrying the very big hat box with the special hat inside.

The wedding day arrived. It was sunny but very windy. 'Oh dear,' she thought, 'how will my hat stay on my head in this wind?' Then she remembered her mother's special box with her beautiful long pins. She fetched it. There were so many different ones – some with pearl beads, some with glass beads and some with silver knobs. She chose the pearl one and pinned her hat to her hair so that, however hard the wind blew, her hat would not blow away.

After the service at the church everyone went to the hotel for the wedding reception. The gardens at the hotel were beautiful – smooth green lawns, lots of beautiful trees and flowers of every colour. There were people there from many countries and the ladies had colourful hats and headwear matching their long flowing dresses. Margaret talked to lots of people and she enjoyed the whole afternoon. She saw some ladies chasing their hats across the lawn, but her special pin kept her hat firmly on her head and the wind was not able to move it.

When she got home she said, 'It was a lovely wedding, and I didn't have to worry about my hat!'

Story books

- *Boots for a Bridesmaid*
- *The Bridesmaid*
- *Katie Morag and the Wedding*
- *The Wedding Tea*

Worship time

Place the wedding cake at one end of the room. Ask the children to choose a 'bride' and a 'groom' and, perhaps, to dress up. Form two processions, led by the bride and groom, which will meet at the wedding cake. Sing a song of celebration, then say prayers for people who have just been married. If the cake is real eat it!

Lights

Aim

To help the children
to understand the
importance of light
in our lives.

73

Preparation

Make sure that the setting is entirely ready before the children arrive for their session.

 ## Setting

- As far as possible darken the room in which you meet by drawing the curtains or covering windows with black paper.
- Set up round the room as many different kinds of lights as possible, bearing in mind safety precautions. (Have a fire blanket handy just in case.)
- Use some of the following: fairy lights, coloured lights, halogen lamp, bedside lamp, spot-light, angle-poise lamp, torches, oil lamps, glow plugs, candles in candle lamps, sulphur rods, slide projector, overhead projector.

 ## Sharing

What is different about our room today? What different kinds of lights can you see? Which ones have you got in your house? Why are lights important? What do we use to light our rooms when the electricity breaks down? What other lights can you think of that are not here?

 # Play

Do not let the children play in the setting. Encourage them to come in together and to sit on the floor looking at everything around them. Have a selection of shapes cut out of card, e.g. lighthouse, aeroplane, house, cat, pillar box, person. (Where possible use shapes which can have holes cut into them for effect, e.g. for eyes in a figure, the light in the lighthouse.) (Fuzzy felt shapes can also be used.) Encourage the children to put the shapes on the overhead projector and to guess what they are.

 # Bible story
LUKE 8.16

'Shall we do the lamps now?' Mary said to Jesus. She knew it was something he liked to help her with. There were so many jobs he couldn't do yet, because he was only a little boy.

First of all they had to gather all the lamps together from the various places in the house where they were used. There was the one in the corner where the water pitcher was kept and one on the shelf where the family put their rolled up beds in the daytime. One lamp was always put on a tiny shelf near the door. Then one lamp went on a tall wooden stand. Joseph had made that lamp stand in his carpenter's workshop. Jesus liked that lamp the best. It stood near where he slept at night. He loved to watch the flickering shadows made by the flame of the lamp as he went to sleep.

The lamps were all lined up in a row so each one could be checked. Mary looked to see if the wick was all right. She used long threads of flax that had to be threaded through the little hole at the top of the lamp. Then it was time for Jesus to pour olive oil, very carefully, into each lamp. The oil level had to be just right, so that the flame would burn steadily and not go out suddenly. Today he did it really well.

They were just putting the lamps back in their right places, when Joseph called from his workshop. 'Can you come and help me for a minute, Jesus, please?' So Jesus put down the lamp, the one that went on the wooden stand, and ran off to help his father.

That evening, as it began to get dark, Mary went round lighting each lamp. She did the one in the corner, the one on the bedding shelf and the one by the door. But where was the lamp that went on the wooden stand? Mary searched all round the little house and couldn't see it anywhere. Then she picked up the big bowl she used for mixing bread, and there was the lamp underneath. 'It won't do much good there,' she said, 'where no one can see it.' The lamp was lit and lifted on to the top of the stand. 'That's better,' said Joseph. 'Now everyone can see its light.'

When Jesus was grown up and he was talking to people about how they should use all their gifts to help other people, he remembered this lamp on its stand and told them they should be like bright lights and not hide the things they are good at and which help other people.

Activities

- Use ready-prepared simple shadow puppets. Set up a screen or sheet with a bright light behind it, e.g. an overhead projector. Encourage the children to create shadows, telling stories, if they wish.

- Mix PVA glue with poster paint. Provide clean jam jars which the children can paint in any way they wish. Put a night-light into each jar. Have a taper available with which to light the lights.

Music and rhymes

SONGS

'A special star' (*BBP*)

'Keep a light in your eyes for the children' (*BBP*)

'This little light of mine' (*JP*)

'Give me oil in my lamp' (*CP*)

'Twinkle, twinkle, little star'

RHYMES

There is no need to light a night-light
On a light night like tonight;
For a night-light's light's a slight light
When the moonlight's white and bright.

Speech Rhymes

(*Use fingers for this rhyme.*)
One birthday candle when you're one year old,
Two birthday candles when you're two years old.
Three when you're three, four when you're four,
All the birthday candles with their flames of gold.

Traditional

Five bright red candles, lighting up the door,
One blew out in the wind, then there were four.

Four bright red candles, lit for birthday tea.
Danny went and blew one out, then there were three.

Three bright red candles, looking very new,
One wouldn't light at all, then there were two.

Two birthday candles, on a sticky bun,
One fell over, then there was one.

One bright red candle, standing in the sun,
It melted right away, then there were none.

Drama and movement

If it is a sunny day, go outside to play 'chasing the shadows'. One group runs about and the others chase their shadows. Pretend to be different kinds of lights, e.g. a candle, a powerful beam.

Another story

'What are we doing tonight?' asked Panish. The family were on holiday by the seaside. It was the first time Panish had ever been to the seaside and he was very excited because he had been on the sand building castles and paddling in the sea. He had also been out in a boat to watch the dolphins playing in the water. This evening he did not know what was planned.

Dad and Mum were talking and Panish was looking out of the window watching the waves bumping into the rocks and splashing white everywhere. Mum and Dad stopped talking and came over to the window and Dad said, 'We thought we would go on the bus along the sea front tonight and look at all the lights.' Panish was very excited by this. The lights had looked fun from the window last night. They seemed to go on for a very long way. Soon they were in the queue for the bus and when it came they went upstairs where there was no roof.

The lights were all different. Panish saw lights that looked like his favourite Disney characters. Ones that looked like animals, flowers and shooting stars. There were lights of every colour and shape, even trains, planes and ships all in lights. Some of the decorations were blowing about in the wind.

There was one very bright light. It was sometimes on and sometimes off and it was further away than the others. Panish asked Dad what it was. 'That's a very special light,' he replied. 'It's in a very tall house which is built on a rock in the water. It's called a lighthouse.' Panish couldn't understand why anyone would want to live in a house on a rock in the sea with no roads and no garden. His dad explained that it was a special house with a special light which was there to stop the sailors crashing ships into the rocks. 'When the light shines on and off the sailors see it and they know that it is rocky and they need to keep away from the light.'

All the way home Panish talked about the lighthouse and said he thought it was better than all the other lights.

Story books
- *Can't You Sleep Little Bear?*
- *Find Out About Light and Sound*
- *Lights*
- *Lights for Gita*
- *Lucy and Tom's ABC*
- *Shine a Light*

Worship time

Put the jam jar lights the children have made on a table in the centre. Light them. Turn off all other lights. Gather around the table. Spend time in quiet. Thank God for light.

Trees

Aim

To discover the beauty, wonder and usefulness of trees.

77

Setting

ON THE WALLS

- Pictures of trees in various seasons.

WOODLAND SETTING

- On a piece of hessian, placed over a shower curtain: fallen branches, twigs, bark, leaves, acorns and conkers.
- In deep flowerpots with wet sand or bricks with holes in or the Scouts' flag stand: pruned branches from different types of trees. Include evergreens.

THINGS WHICH GROW ON TREES

- Apples, pears, coconut, bananas, acorns, conkers, dates, figs, safe berries, blossom, etc.

IN A SEPARATE AREA

- Bonsai trees, miniature trees and decorated branches.

Sharing

What do you think we're talking about today? Where do trees grow? What do we call places where there are lots of trees? Why do we have trees? What makes its home in a tree? Encourage the children to explore the setting and everything in it

Bible story
LUKE 19.1–10

There were so many people in the square and they all seemed very excited. Ezz, Tabitha's brother, was sitting on the flat roof of the house. He had seen the square with people in it before but never as many people as today. They were not only in the square but also on either side of the road leading into the square. 'Why are they here?' he thought. 'It's not the fish barrow today.' Ezz liked the fish barrow day when the fishermen brought their catch to sell and all the people came to buy. He loved to see all the different coloured fish and some days his mother bought fish for supper. 'Why are they here?' he said to himself.

Whatever was going on! Across the road there were some sycamore trees and there was someone climbing one of them. Ezz looked twice – he couldn't believe what he was seeing. It was Zac, who was not a very popular person in the village. He was a tax man and everyone said he always took too much tax money, so that he could keep lots for himself. He couldn't believe Zac was climbing up into the sycamore tree. He was a very small man, so if he was not in the front row in a crowd he would not see very much. He was obviously wanting to see what was going on. It must be something very special.

It wasn't long before something happened. Lots of men were coming down the road. One of them stood out as being different. The men came into the square and stopped to talk to everyone. The crowd listened while the special man spoke. They all seemed very interested.

Then it happened! – the big surprise of the day. The man walked towards the sycamore tree, stopped underneath it and looked up. He called to Zac to come down and said he wanted to go to his house for tea. 'Why ever would he want to do that?' thought Ezz. 'No one likes Zac.'

Zac came down the tree. He looked very shocked and surprised. Zac and the man they called Jesus walked off down the road.

The next day Zac came into the village and gave money to everyone he had taken too much from. He said he had promised Jesus he would never cheat again.

Ezz was astonished – Zac was so different. Jesus must have changed him.

Activities

- If it is the appropriate season, stick (with PVA glue) leaves on to sheets of paper. 'Paint' with a dilute form of PVA glue to preserve and make shiny.
- Printing with wooden shapes.
- Simple bark rubbings.
- Use twigs and sticks to build little houses, bridges, etc. Use with small models of people.
- Go for a walk and let the children feel different trees and tree trunks but instil the country code so that they do not damage the trees.

Music and rhymes

SONGS

'Just a tiny seed' (*BBP*)

'Who put the white in the clouds?' (*BBP*)

'God made the heavens and earth' (verse 3) (*BBP*)

'How beautiful' (*BBP*)

'Zacchaeus was a very little man' (*JP*)

'Neath the spreading chestnut tree' (*Okki Tokki Unga*)

'Thank you Lord' (*CP*)

RHYMES

'Here is a tree with its leaves so green' (*This Little Puffin*)

In the middle of the wood
all alone a beech tree stood,
doing what a beech tree should,
blowing in the wind!

One little leaf came tumbling down,
tumbling down, tumbling down.
One little leaf came tumbling down
and landed on the ground.

One little owl flew around, etc.

One little squirrel jumped around, etc.

One little mouse scampered around, etc.

One little rabbit hopped around, etc.

One little hedgehog shuffled around, etc.
and sat down on the ground.

Five Furry Teddy Bears

Here beside the hedge I stand,
with an acorn in my hand.
Folded small as small may be,
in the acorn lies a tree.

A Word in Season

We are lovely chestnut trees,
Leaves are shaking in the breeze.
See us stand so straight and high
Looking upwards to the sky.
Wave our branches to and fro.
Then make shade for flowers below.

Finger Plays and Rhymes

Drama and movement

Mime trees growing, moving in the breeze, moving in a gale, crashing to the ground, being chopped down.

Another story

'Come on everyone, time to be off,' said Dad. 'Have you all got your woolly hats and scarves?'

'Why do we need them on a lovely sunny warm day like today?' asked Laura.

Dad looked mysterious. 'You'll find out,' he said. They all went outside to get in the car, but to the children's surprise it was Mum's car they were using. 'What's happening today?' Ben asked. 'You usually laugh at Mum's little car, Dad. You call it a two-horse model!' 'Not today,' Dad replied. 'It will be perfect for what we are going to do.'

'What's that anyway?' asked the children. Mum explained that they were going to buy a present for Gran and Grandad for their new flat. 'We want to give them a little garden they can look after and grow on the balcony there,' she said. 'They have always grown flowers and vegetables and they both love trees so much.'

'Trees on a balcony,' said Ben. 'That sounds impossible.' 'Just wait and see,' said Dad.

At the garden centre, they got a great big trolley to push around and collect all the things they needed. They chose some bulbs to put in pots and lots of small plants to grow in the window boxes they found. There were long pots, called troughs, and Mum picked out packets of lettuce and radish seeds to plant in them. The trolley was getting full of bags of special soil, pots of all sizes and shapes and the plants.

'Now for the trees!' said Dad. 'We'll have to go outside to find them.' It was almost like a miniature forest out there in the tree corner of the garden centre. There were short fat prickly trees, taller bushy ones tied up in string bags, even tiny baby Christmas trees. 'It's apple trees we are looking for,' said Mum. 'We need two of them so they'll have apples in a few years' time.' Laura and Ben looked at each other and laughed. 'How can you grow apples on the balcony of a flat?' they wondered.

When they had chosen two special apple trees, like very tall thin broomsticks, Dad lifted them into the trolley. They found two huge pots for the trees and more bags of the right soil for these trees, then they went off to pay for everything.

Next it was time to load it all into the car. 'Now I know why we've come in Mum's car,' said Laura, 'and why we've got our woolly hats and scarves too.' The children watched Dad and Mum roll back part of the roof of her car and fasten it down. Ben and Laura climbed on to the back seat and Dad very carefully lifted the two trees down through the open roof so they could each hold one. The plants and pots and bags of soil were packed in around them.

'Let's put on our hats and scarves before we set off,' said Mum. 'We'll be going very slowly, so the trees don't get broken in the wind, and it will be cold.' It wasn't very far to the new flat, which was a good thing as it certainly was a windy drive. Gran and Grandad were so excited and pleased when their garden arrived. 'I never thought we'd be able to have apple trees again,' said Grandad. 'And maybe some apples one day!' said Gran.

Story books
- *The Brave Ones*
- *The Trunk*
- *Why Do Sunflowers Face the Sun?*

Worship time

Ask the children to collect something from the setting to bring and place in the centre. Sing 'Just a tiny seed', with the children echoing the words.

Bread

Aim

To help the children discover the value of bread as a staple food for many people.

Preparation

Old shower curtain for floor covering.

Setting

THE BAKERY

Bags of flour, large mixing bowls, small bowls of flour, measuring jugs, water, salt, yeast, aprons, wooden boards, bread tins and flat baking tins, scales, spoons (large and small), ears of corn, lumps of self-raising flour dough (see Appendix for recipe) wrapped in cling film.

THE BAKER'S SHOP

A variety of small loaves and bread rolls, paper or plastic bags, a till, money, baskets, purses.

Sharing

Handle a lump of bread dough and ask the children if they know who you are pretending to be.

What does a baker do? What does he do to make the bread? What different kinds of bread do you know? What other things do bakers make?

Where does flour come from? (Show the corn ears and talk about where they grow.)

Encourage the children to use the setting and everything in it to play at shopkeepers and bakers.

Bible story

JOHN 6.1–14

'Mum! Mum! Where are you?' Ben ran round the house looking for his mother. He must find her and he didn't know where she was. He ran into the garden and there she was talking to the lady next door 'Mum!' he shouted. 'I've been looking for you everywhere. Melach and Joe are going on a hike over the hills. Can I go with them and can I take a packed lunch, please?'

His mother, seeing there was no more peace, said goodbye to her friend and asked what all the fuss was about. 'Please, Mum, can I go with them?'

Mum said he could go if he was sensible, and they went to get his food ready. Ben had said he would like some of his favourite little loaves, the ones that were like rolls, and some sardines. His mother said she had five loaves but there were only two sardines left. Ben was happy to have the two fish and all five rolls. So they packed his rucksack and he took an orange and a flask of water.

'Goodbye, Mum,' he said and off he went to meet the others.

They set off towards the lakeside – they liked watching the boats and the fishermen. There were lots of boats on the water and the fishermen kept hauling in the nets which sparkled in the sun. Melach said that it was the silver fish that were sparkling.

Joe and Melach said they were hungry so they sat on the lakeside and ate their lunch but Ben only wanted his orange. He decided he would save his rolls and fish for later.

There seemed to be a lot of people on the path ahead of them, all climbing the hill. Ben and Joe thought it would be fun to follow them and see where they were going. Melach agreed and they all set off up the hill.

When they reached the top there were so many people, thousands of them, all sitting on the ground and there seemed to be someone at the front who was speaking to them.

Ben was curious, so he persuaded the others go with him, weaving their way to the front of the crowd to find out what it was all about.

They stepped over lots of legs, reached the front and sat down to listen. The man seemed very nice and he had a lovely smile. Soon after they got to the front he stopped speaking. His friends gathered round him and Joe overheard them saying that they thought the people were hungry. The nice man asked his friends if they had any food for the people. The friends looked at each other and shook their heads. 'Has anyone in the crowd got any food?' he asked. 'Go and see.' Joe nudged Ben and said 'You've still got yours. Shall I tell them?' 'No,' said Ben 'there is only enough for me and I want it, I'm hungry.'

The men started looking around and asking if anyone had any food. Ben was quiet at first. Then he thought he ought to tell them, but he couldn't believe that his five barley loaves and two sardines would be any use when there were thousands of people.

Ben took his food up to one of the men who seemed excited that there was some food and took it to the nice man. He said a prayer and told his friends to take the food and share it with everybody. To Ben's amazement there was enough food for the three of them and for everybody else.

The nice man thanked Ben for being so generous. Ben asked him what his name was so that he could tell his mum when he got home. 'My name is Jesus,' the man said. Ben remembered that he had heard about this man doing good things. He said that this would be a special day, a day he would remember all his life.

Activities

- Make bread (quick method in Appendix, see page 106).
- Make sandwiches or rolls.
- Make toast with a toaster.
- Make toasted sandwiches with a sandwich maker.

Music and rhymes

SONGS

'Pat a cake, pat a cake' (Traditional)

'Five little loaves' (*CP*)

'From hand to hand' (*BBP*)

'Five currant buns in a baker's shop' (*This Little Puffin*)

Let's pretend to make some bread
Make some bread – make some bread
Let's pretend to make some bread
On this (Sunday) morning.

First of all we weigh the flour . . .

Now we have to add the yeast . . .

Let us pour some water in . . .

Bump and thump and knead the dough . . .

Put the bread in the oven to bake . . .

Cut and spread the bread to eat . . .

Five Furry Teddy Bears

Rhymes

Tea time

Tea time, tea time,

Come and have your tea

Bread and butter,

Cakes and jam for me,

I've had my bread and butter,

I've drunk my cup of tea.

What is there for supper?

Wait and see.

Finger Plays and Rhymes

Drama and movement

Act out 'Let's pretend to make some bread' (see p. 83).

Another story

'I like coming into this shop, Mummy. The bread always smells so lovely.' All round them there were racks of bread. Some were very flat. Mummy told them that they were called pitta bread and that they were special to people from Greece. The strong smelling bread was called naan and that was special to people from Asia. There were some lovely big shiny loaves like brown rocks. They had little seeds on the top and they were special to people from Cyprus. They then spotted some very dark brown pudding-like bread and Mummy explained it was rye bread and a favourite with German people. Bridget saw the very long thin loaves and said she knew that they came from France.

'Look at the piggy-back loaves,' said Bridget. Mummy explained they were called cottage loaves and they were easy to make at home. 'In fact,' said Mummy, 'we could make some this afternoon. We need to add yeast and bread flour to our shopping list.'

The girls were so excited at the thought of making cottage loaves that they helped to do the shopping in double quick time. Then it was off home to make bread.

They put the flour to warm while they had lunch and then they put on their cooking aprons. Mummy got the bowls out and warmed some milk. The girls helped to mix the yeast with sugar and warm milk. They stirred it well until it was smooth and runny. It had an unusual smell and it started to bubble.

Next they made a hole in the middle of the flour, and took it in turns to pour in the yeast and milk. It was fun! They put their clean hands in and mixed the sticky dough. It was a funny feeling and it made them giggle as they mixed it.

Mummy divided the dough into two bowls and covered them with a cloth and put them in a warm place. They peeped every few minutes and watched the dough getting bigger.

'Now it is time to be rough with it,' said Mummy. They each had a floured board and turned out their bowl of dough. They punched it and banged it. It made a wonderful sound. Mummy showed them how to make smooth balls and they each made a big and a small ball.

They brushed milk on the bottom one and put the little one on top. They pushed their longest fingers down through the middle. 'I've done it,' said Pat. 'It's a piggy-back loaf! I can't wait until it's cooked.'

Story books
- *Bread*, 1990
- *Bread*, 1991

Worship time

Have a basket of small rolls, sufficient for everyone. Stand or sit in a circle. Ask one of the children to give a roll to each of the others, as you play the music and then sing the first verse of 'From hand to hand' (*BBP*).

Wheels

Setting

Wheel shapes fastened to wall/display board. Create settings in different areas:

VEHICLE WHEELS

- Tricycle, small bicycle, etc.
- Ride-on toddler's vehicle.
- Other ride-on vehicles.
- Toy cars, lorries, etc.
- Road track for running them on.
- Steering wheel.

WHEELS AT HOME

- Tea trolley.
- Wheelbarrow.
- Mower.
- Hoover/vacuum cleaner.
- Pram, push chair.
- Pastry wheel.
- Pizza wheel.
- Rotary whisk.
- Pastry, lattice, tracing and icing wheels.
- Carriage clock with wheels showing.
- Pocket watches with open backs (not valuable antiques).

OTHER WHEELS

- Potter's wheel.
- Spinning wheel.
- Picture of ferris wheel ('big' wheel).
- Wheels for hamsters and gerbils.

TOY WHEELS

- Wheels for water and sand play.
- Duplo.
- Lego.
- Junior Meccano, Brio, etc.
- Building set with wheels.

Sharing

What do you think we are going to talk about today? What have you got in your house that has wheels? Why do some things need wheels? How many wheels has a car?

What else has four wheels? What has more than four wheels? What has two wheels? Can you think of anything with one wheel?

Encourage the children to discover and play with everything in the setting.

Bible story
JOHN 4.6–10

Jesus was hot, tired and very thirsty. He was travelling through a country called Samaria. The people there, the Samaritans, had been the enemies of his country for a very long time. People from Jesus' country and the Samaritans didn't speak to each other.

Jesus was on his own. It was the middle of the day. He came to a well and sat beside it. He was too tired to bother to turn the wheel to let down the bucket into the well, but he was longing for a drink.

He was surprised to see a woman walking to the well with a water pot on her head. Why was she coming to the well in the hot sun, rather than in the morning or the evening when the sun was not making it so hot? As he watched her she started to turn the handle on the wheel to let the bucket down. When it had gone deep enough to fill up with water she turned the wheel the other way to pull it up. Soon there was a bucket full of clear, sparkling water.

Jesus said to her, 'Please may I have a drink?' The woman was astonished and said, 'Nobody from your country talks to someone from mine! They never share a drink of water.' Jesus said he really would like a drink. They talked together for a long time. Jesus enjoyed the cool, fresh sparkling water that she gave him and he felt refreshed by it. They continued to talk and the more they talked the more the Samaritan woman realized that he was someone special, someone sent from God. When he had gone she ran back to her village to tell everyone about him. She even forgot her waterpot!

Activities

- Do wheel-painting. Run wheels or small vehicles through trays with pieces of foam soaked in paint. Use the wheels to make patterns.
- Use construction kits which include plenty of wheels.
- Make a collage with wheel-shaped pasta.

Music and rhymes

SONGS

'God has put a circle round us' (*BBP*)

'Riding in a car on the motorway' (*BBP*)

'The wheels on the bus go round and round' (*Okki Tokki Unga*)

'Wheels keep turning' (*Apusskidu*)

RHYMES

'Let's all ride our bicycles' (*see* **Roads**, *page 91*)

Um-pa-pa, um-pa-pa,
let's pay our fare.
Um-pa-pa, um-pa-pa,
strapped in our chair.
Ready to fly like a bird in the air,
when we are at the fair.

Um-pa-pa, um-pa-pa,
feel the wheel go.
Um-pa-pa, um-pa-pa,
look down below.
Let's give a wave to the people we know,
when we are at the fair.

Five Furry Teddy Bears

One wheel on a barrow,
Painted red and blue
Two wheels on my scooter
And on my cycle too.
Three wheels on a tricycle
But that's too small for me.
Four wheels on a motor car
As anyone can see.

Finger Plays and Rhymes

The aeroplane taxies down the field
And heads into the breeze,
It lifts its wheels above the ground,
It skims above the trees.
It rises high and higher,
Away up toward the sun,
It's just a speck against the sky –
And now it's gone.

Knock at the Door

John rides on a bicycle,
Ringing ting-a-ling.
Tommy has a tricycle,
Rattling old thing.
Polly has a pedal car,
Toot, toot goes the hooter,
But I'm the fastest of them all
A-scooting on my scooter.

Jenny pushes her doll's pram
Full of tatty teddies.
Peter pulls his painted horse,
Shouting 'Gee up Neddy'.
Dougie drags a wobbly train,
Hoot, hoot goes the hooter.
But I'm the fastest of them all,
A-scooting on my scooter.

Helter Skelter

Drama and movement

Make wheel movements with hands, wrists, arms, fingers, legs and ankles. Make them large and small, fast and slow, smooth and jerky.

Another story

'What are we going to do today?' said Karen. She, her brother Tom and their mum were on holiday in the Isle of Wight. They were having a lovely time. Mum had driven their car on to the ferry boat and they had sailed across the water to Yarmouth. During the week they had been to different beaches, one with brown sand, one where the sand seemed to go on for miles, one where the sand was many different colours. They had also had adventures at Robin Hill and been to a funfair. 'But,' said Karen, 'what are we going to do today?'

'There's a special place we must go,' said mum. 'It's called Carisbrooke Castle.' So they went. It was a big, exciting, ruined castle where there were lots of places to climb. It was also very interesting. They heard how a king called Charles the First had been a prisoner there when the people were angry with him and how he tried to escape.

They were sitting on a bench, eating their lunch, when they saw a man walk by leading a donkey. 'Oh, Mum, please can I have a donkey ride?' asked Tom. 'That donkey's not for riding,' said Mum, 'it's got an important job to do.' 'Let's go and see.' They followed the man and the donkey into a building. Lots of other people had also come to see what was happening. In the building was a great, big, wooden wheel. It was much bigger than a big lorry's wheels; in fact it was taller than a lorry! As soon as she saw the wheel the donkey knew just what to do. She climbed inside it and stood, waiting very patiently. The man gave her an order and the donkey started to walk slowly inside the wheel. As she walked on the wooden track the wheel began to turn. The more she walked, the more the wheel turned. 'What a clever donkey,' said Karen, 'but why is she doing it?' 'Look carefully, listen and wait and see,' said Mum. They heard a banging noise, they saw there was a great, thick rope fastened to the wheel, they saw that there was a large hole going deep into the ground. Then they saw that on the end of the rope there was an enormous bucket, full of water. 'It's a well!' shouted Tom. 'How clever,' said Karen. 'As the donkey treads the wheel to make it turn it pulls up the bucket. What fun.' 'It's fun for us to watch,' said Mum, 'but when people lived in the castle it was the only way they could get their water from the very deep well. The king who was a prisoner here drank water pulled up by a donkey.' 'Do you think it was the donkey's grandpa who pulled up water for the king?' asked Tom. Mum smiled. 'It was a very long time ago,' she said, 'but it might have been her great, great, great, great, great, great, great, great (everyone joins in) grandpa.'

Story books

- *Are We There Yet?*
- *Cars*
- *Let's Look at Things That Go*
- *Morton Gets Set*
- *Mr Gumpy's Motor Car*
- *Mrs Armitage on Wheels*
- *My Bike*

Worship time

For each person tie a metre length of tape or ribbon to a hoop for use in the prayer time. Ask someone to stand in the centre of the group, holding the hoop, to be the hub of the wheel. Everyone else stands in a circle, each holding a tape to represent the spokes of the wheel. Sing 'God has put a circle round us', verses 1 and 2, moving round as you do so.

Roads

Aim

To help children to be aware, not only of the usefulness of roads, but of the need for everyone to take care, both of themselves and of other people.

Setting

IN ONE AREA

A road play mat, with model cars, garage, etc.

IN A SECOND AREA

Toy cars made from cardboard boxes, old tyres, etc.

IN A THIRD AREA

A zebra crossing, beacons (made from long cardboard tubes and orange balloons or plastic footballs), a 'lollipop' pole and yellow fluorescent jacket, a set of traffic lights (made from a pole with cardboard boxes).

ON THE WALLS AND ON A TABLE

Maps and books of maps, photocopied driving licences, wall-mounted road signs.

IN THE BACKGROUND

Play a tape of road noises recorded locally.

Sharing

How did you get here? What did you come in? What did it travel on? What different kinds of roads do we have? What do you have to remember when you are crossing the road?

Use the setting and everything in it.

Bible story

MARK 11.1–10

'Come and see this, Tobias,' said Nathan. 'There are two people walking along our street; they're peering round every corner. They seem to be looking for something. I wonder what it is!'

As the men got nearer, the boys could hear them talking to each other. 'Jesus said we'd find a young donkey tied up outside a house in this village, but so far, I've only seen really old donkeys,' said one of the men. The other one replied 'We've a bit further to go yet, and we'll ask these boys if they can help us.'

Nathan and Tobias felt quite important. 'We've got a little donkey,' said Nathan. 'It's tied up in the shade of the big tree, behind our house. Come and have a look, if you like.' 'Why do you want a donkey?' asked Tobias. He loved this donkey, and he was a bit worried. 'I hope you're not going to take it away from us,' he said.

'Do you think you could find your father for us?' said the tall man. 'We'll explain it all then.'

Tobias raced round to his father's workshop. 'You'd better come quickly, Dad; two men want our donkey,' he told him. Dad followed Tobias to meet these men. 'Now what's all this about?' he said. 'You've quite upset my little boy!'

'I'm Andrew, and this is Philip,' said one of the men. 'We are friends of Jesus, and he's sent us to find a young donkey that he can ride into the big city of Jerusalem.' 'Yes,' said Philip, 'and he told us that if we said to the donkey's owner that the Lord had need of it and would send it back when he'd finished with it, the owner would understand.' The boys' father smiled. 'I've been expecting you,' he said. 'I was reading the book of Zechariah last night and it spoke of this. Somehow I knew my donkey would be needed.' He patted his little donkey, untied the rope and gave it to Philip. 'Come on, boys,' he said. 'We'll go with them.'

Nathan and Tobias were really excited now. They kept running ahead and then back again along the road. After a while they could hear a lot of shouting and saw a crowd of people waving things in the air.

Then they saw Jesus, standing quietly with his friends, waiting for Andrew and Philip with the donkey. He had such a kind face and it broke into a lovely smile when he saw the little donkey. 'Thank you very much for lending me your special donkey,' he said to the boys' father and he stroked the donkey's head very gently. 'You'll look after it well, won't you?' Nathan asked anxiously. 'We all love it so much.'

Jesus told the boys not to worry and he asked them to walk beside him. 'The donkey knows you,' he said, 'so it won't be so nervous with all this shouting.' Nathan and Tobias never forgot that walk along the road into Jerusalem. It was like going through a forest. Lots of people had cut palm branches off the trees at the side of the road and they waved them over Jesus, the donkey, the boys and Jesus' friends.

At the end of the walk, Jesus got off the donkey's back. He patted it and gave it back to the family. 'You've helped us a lot today,' he said. 'Thank you very much.'

Activities

● Make a road collage or montage using pictures cut from magazines or the children's drawings.
● Play in the setting again.
● Go for a walk to see cars, buses, etc.
● Make traffic light biscuits (see biscuit recipe in Appendix, page 105). Make round biscuits, half of which have three holes cut in them using an apple-corer. Cook. Fasten a cut biscuit to each uncut biscuit with pre-prepared butter icing. Fill the holes with dabs of strawberry jam, apricot jam or lemon curd, and lime marmalade.

Music and rhymes

SONGS

'Riding in a car on the motorway' (*BBP*)

'First of all we'll dig a hole'
(*for full text see page 35*)

When you want to cross the road, cross the road,
Find a policeman if you can, if you can.
Tell him nicely what you want –
He is such a helpful man, helpful man.

When the traffic's safely stopped, safely stopped.
and the policeman's said 'Right oh, right oh!'
Look both ways, then walk across,
While it is safe to go, safe to go.
(*Sing to the tune of 'Heads and shoulders'.*)
Five Furry Teddy Bears

RHYMES

Let's all ride our bicycles,
pedalling fast then slow.
Riding up and down the road,
watch us as we go.

Let's all drive our motor cars,
sometimes fast then slow.
Driving up and down the road,
watch us as we go.

Let's all drive our lorries now,
when empty fast – then slow.
Carrying concrete up the road,
watch us as we go.

Five Furry Teddy Bears

Drama and movement

Act out various ways of travelling on a road – walking, running, roller-blading, scooting, etc.

Pretend to travel on the road using various forms of transport, e.g. cars, bicycles, tractors, horses, camels.

Act out making and mending roads.

Another story

'This is a boring road,' came a voice from the back of the car. 'Will we be on it for much longer?' Tom was fed up. Usually he liked going on journeys, because there was so much to see, but today they were on a big wide motorway and all he could see were big lorries and coaches whizzing past. Baby Holly was fast asleep in the car seat beside him and Dad seemed to be nodding off too. Mum was driving and she said the road was so busy that she couldn't manage to talk as well as drive.

But when he heard Tom, Dad sat up and looked at the map. 'In a few minutes, Tom, we'll see a big blue and white notice with a number on it,' he said. 'If it's No.8 we turn off on to a different road, so keep a good lookout'. Tom sat up and watched. Sure enough, there it was, No.8 on the big blue notice. 'Thank goodness,' said Mum. 'I'll be really glad to get off this busy motorway. Let's hope the next road will be quieter.' They turned off on to another big road but there was more to see and not so much traffic. Dad said it was called a dual carriageway because there were two roads side by side for things going in different directions. They were all on their way to stay with Mark and Ruth, and their parents who used to live next door to them. 'The next thing to look out for, Tom,' said Mum, 'is a sign with a crossed knife and fork on it. That will mean it's a good place to stop and stretch our legs and have a drink.' After a few more bends and up and down a hill, there it was. 'Hooray!' Tom called out. 'My legs are ready for some stretching!' After this little rest, Dad took over the driving. He said we must look out for a sign, like a white finger, showing the way to Willowbank. 'Is that where Mark and Ruth live?' asked Tom. 'No. But once we are there I can start to use the map that Mark and Ruth's dad sent us.' 'Here's the sign,' Mum said. 'We turn left here.' It was not a very wide road and it wasn't as straight as the dual carriageway, but it was much more interesting. They passed farms with cows and sheep in the fields and there was a huge red tractor waiting by a gate, to come out on to their road.

'I'm glad we are in front of that tractor,' said Dad. 'We'd have to go really slowly behind him on this winding road.' They went on through the village of Willowbank, looking for their next turn. It was a very narrow road. 'If this road gets any smaller,' said Tom anxiously, 'there won't be room for our car.' He couldn't see very much because of the high hedges either side, but it was quite exciting wondering what was round the next bend. They all laughed when they found Hillside Lane where Mark and Ruth lived. It was just as narrow, went up a steep hill and had grass growing down the middle! But there was the cottage they were looking for and there were Mark and Ruth on the look out. 'What a journey,' said Dad, 'and what a lot of different roads we've been on.'

Story books
- *Impo*
- *Let's Look at Things That Go*

 ## Worship time

Go to the setting for final prayers. Use a verse or two of 'Riding in a car on the motorway' (*BBP*) to run around and then slow down (as directed). Thank God for good careful drivers and people who make and look after roads.

Pots and pans

Aim

To develop an awareness of the skills used in making pots and pans and the practical uses to which they are put.

Setting
MEAL TIME

Have a table with a cloth on laid with cups, saucers, plates, jug, mugs, teapot, etc. (Recognize that in some parts of the country these utensils are referred to as pots.)

METAL ITEMS

Saucepans, frying pans, kettle for the stove, metal casserole dishes, wok, omelette pan, poacher, grill pan, baking trays, etc. (Provide a large cardboard box to act as a cooker.)

PLASTIC CONTAINERS

Basins, bowls, food canisters, mugs, child's plastic pot.

OUTDOOR ITEMS

Put on a piece of green plastic grass: plastic and clay flowerpots, garden pots.

Sharing

What are pots and pans? What's the same about all pots and pans? What's different about them? What are they made of? Why are they made of different things? Which of them do you have in your house? What are they used for?

Use the setting and everything in it to play pretend games, e.g. tossing pancakes, making cakes, doing the gardening, having tea.

Bible story
MARK 14.12–16

'I must have eaten something that upset me yesterday.' Naomi wasn't feeling very well and she was not feeling well enough to be able to do the things she would normally do each day. She would normally have had a very busy day washing the clothes by the stream, cooking for the family, brushing out the house and mending the clothes. The other job which was very important, and had to be done every day, was the fetching of the water.

Naomi and Micah did not have any taps in their house, not even out in the garden. They had to walk to the other side of the village, to the village well, where everybody took their water pots to fetch the water they needed to wash themselves, clean the house, do the cooking and drink.

Naomi normally went every day, carrying her very big stone water pot on her head. She had a special woollen ring which she put on her head and the water pot balanced on it. It was very heavy when it was full but she carried it without spilling the water. Naomi enjoyed going to the village well because she met the other women from the village and they shared their family news.

Today she had promised to help Sarah who had to prepare her upper room for visitors and she needed an extra pot of water. Naomi had said that as they would not need one for themselves today she would fetch Sarah's extra water.

She was not well enough to go to the well and so she asked Micah if he would go to fetch the water. He was not very happy at first because he said that it was not a job that men did and he didn't want to be seen walking through the village with a water pot on his head. When he realized how sick Naomi was he said he would go, otherwise Sarah would not have enough water.

Jesus was staying in the area and he and his friends were going to have a meal together. Jesus asked two of the disciples to go and get the room ready. 'Make sure there is water and a towel and bowl, and bread and wine. It would be best if we all sat around one table and then we can all share together.' The disciples agreed and then asked 'How shall we know where the room is?' 'That is not a problem. You will see a man carrying a pitcher of water. Follow him.' 'A man carrying a pitcher of water!' said Thomas, 'Yes, that is unusual I know but it will be a man,' said Jesus.

The disciples set off into the village and sure enough they saw the man with the pitcher and they followed him. He finally climbed some stairs into a long room. There was a woman there, who greeted the man whom she called Micah. She thanked him for bringing the water and asked how Sarah was. She knew his wife was not well.

The men stood in the doorway watching and listening. Then Sarah saw them and said, 'You must be the Man from Galilee's friends. I hope the room is the way you want it and you have everything you need.' They remembered what Jesus had said. They looked around and everything was fine. They thanked Sarah and Micah and returned to join the other disciples so that they could show them the way to their evening meal.

Activities

- Use Newclay to make pots.
- Use Plasticine or salt dough to make coil pots.
- Decorate flowerpots with sponge painting using small pieces of sponge dipped into a mixture of ready-mixed paint and PVA glue.
- Plant seeds in small flowerpots. (Nasturtium seeds are a good size and grow quickly.)
- Do some cooking.

Music and rhymes

SONGS

'Polly put the kettle on' (*Puffin Book of Nursery Rhymes*)

'Give me oil in my lamp' (*JP*)

'I'm a little tea pot' (Traditional, from *This Little Puffin*)

'Five fat sausages frying in a pan' (*This Little Puffin*)

'I like eating' (*BBP*)

Add the following verse:
I like helping (*echo*)
Getting jobs done (*echo*)
Washing up with Daddy (*echo*)
Cooking with my mum. (*echo*)
Planting seeds (*echo*)
Pulling up the weeds (*echo*)
Thank you God for fun. (*echo*)

RHYMES

'Find a spark, light the fire' (*Five Furry Teddy Bears*, see p. 16 for full text)

Pancakes, pancakes, pancakes for tea.
Who'd like to make some pancakes with me?
We'll mix them and beat them
And toss them once more.
Oh no! Mine's just landed face down on
    the floor.

Five Furry Teddy Bears

I knew a man who always wore
A saucepan on his head.
I asked him what he did it for –
'I don't know why,' he said.
It always makes my ears so sore;
I should have left it off before
And worn a frying-pan.

Speech Rhymes

Drama and movement

Act out all the things involved in being a potter:

Carry in the heavy sack of clay.

Break off pieces of clay into lumps.

Throw lumps on to the bench.

Pummel and shape it.

Roll it into long sausages.

Spin the potter's wheel.

Shape the pot.

Carry the pot very carefully.

Another story

'Reena, Reena, come quickly. Look at this lovely silver trail,' said Neil. Reena and Neil were helping Mum with the gardening and Neil had been sorting the flowerpots into different sizes. He had just found a big one with silver twisting lines across it. Reena ran across the garden and as they were looking at the trail and looked to see where it came from, they found a very large snail which was slithering across the bottom of the pot.

Mummy had come to see what was so interesting. She told them that snails loved walking on earthenware pots. She put two pots close to each other and the snail moved from one to the other and left another trail.

'These pots are not like the ones we brought our plants home in from the garden centre, are they?' Mum told them that the ones from the garden centre were plastic and the others were made from earthenware. 'What is earthenware?' asked Reena. Mum explained that it was a clay which was dug from the earth and washed. 'It can be shaped and baked in a very hot oven. It is very hard then and can often hold water. We have lots of pots indoors made from different kinds of clay. Let's leave the snail playing on the flowerpot and go in for tea and see how many pots we can find in the house.'

Story books

- *Let's Look at Kitchens*
- *Moving House*
- *Moving Molly*
- *My Dad Is Wizard*
- *My Gran Is Great*
- *My Mum Is Magic*
- *My Sister Is Super*
- *Noisy*

Worship time

Put a nightlight into a clay lamp or an aromatherapy container. Gather round the light. Talk about all the people who use their hands to make things. Ask God to bless them.

Look and listen

Setting

LOOKING

- A flower arrangement or some other visual focus.
- Pairs of glasses – reading glasses, distance glasses, bifocals, sunglasses, etc. Books with different sizes of print to look at through the glasses.
- Telescope and binoculars. If possible use the opportunity to go outside to look through them.
- Magnifying glass, insect inspector/viewer, magnifying pot, bug-viewer. Small objects, mini-beasts and books to look at.
- Kaleidoscopes of different kinds, including, if possible, one with lenses which enable the environment to be looked at in patterns.
- An eye-patch, a blindfold as used on airlines, scarves to use for blindfolds.
- Coloured acetate filters, smoked glass.

LISTENING

- A walkman, a portable radio, a stereo-cassette player (use those made for children if possible). Suitable tapes and CDs.
- A collection of whistles, including, if possible, a dog whistle.
- Football rattles, both wooden and plastic (if you can face it!), a bicycle bell and horn.
- A musical box, kitchen timer, ticking and chiming clock, wind chimes.
- Bells and percussion instruments. Ethnic instruments, a tuning fork. Chime bars.
- A hearing aid.

Sharing

What can you hear? What sounds came from outside the room? What can you hear inside the room? What are the loudest and softest things you can hear? What are the highest and lowest? What would be difficult if you could not hear? (Be sensitive to anyone with a hearing disability.)

What can you see as you look around? (Adapt the questions to your context, e.g. How many windows are there? What colour is the door? What is under the table?) What would it be like if you could not see? (Be particularly sensitive if you have anyone in the group who has a visual impairment.)

Use everything in the setting for creative play.

Bible story

LUKE 22.15

This is a simple way to tell children how our special service, Holy Communion, comes from the story of the Last Supper.

It would be useful to have a chalice/goblet and a paten/plate and, possibly, one of the famous pictures of the Last Supper.

'This is good,' said Jesus to his disciples. 'We are all here tonight, sitting round the table to have our supper together.' He explained to them that it was going to be a very important time for them all. 'I want you to look and listen and remember everything we say and do this evening,' he said.

First of all they said a prayer, asking God to bless them and the food they were going to eat. It was just like us saying grace before we eat our dinner.

Then Jesus took the plate of bread and shared it out between them all. 'Every time you eat bread you'll remember our meal tonight,' he said, 'even when I'm not here any more.' Later on a cup of wine was passed round from one person to another. Jesus said that they would remember this as well. Everyone was very quiet and thoughtful as all this was happening. They had looked and listened very carefully and they would remember it all.

Activities

- Record familiar sounds on to a cassette (e.g. tap running, car starting up, toilet flushing, front door bell ringing, music of children's TV favourites). Ask children to identify the sounds.

- Make a 'telephone' using two baked bean tins or margarine tubs, stretching a piece of string tautly between them.
- Use some objects which can be opened or cut to reveal something different. Ask the children to look at them carefully, guessing what they are like inside before they are further investigated, and to describe what they will find (e.g. Russian dolls, a firm cabbage, a fresh and a hard-boiled egg, a pomegranate or other unfamiliar fruit, a kiwi fruit).
- Go outside to look and listen.
- Look at a few slides, e.g. holiday, another country, flowers, etc.
- Play hide and seek.

Music and rhymes

SONGS

'He gave us eyes that we may see' (*JP*)

'Two little eyes' (*JP*)

'Who made your eyes?' (*BBP*)

'The wheels on the bus' (*Okki Tokki Unga*)

'From hand to hand' (*BBP*)

'I have seen the golden sunshine' (*Someone's Singing, Lord*)

'God has given us eyes to see, let's look' (*BBP*)
Use first verse, then insert the following verse:

God has given us ears to hear, let's listen!
God has given us ears to hear, let's listen!
Let's listen and hear what is happening in
   the world around,
Let's listen.
Let's listen and hear what is happening in
   the world around.
Let's listen and hear.

'Playing, running, skipping, jumping!' (*BBP*)

Add the following verse:
Looking, watching, hearing, listening,
Super things to do!
And I like them best when I am
Doing them with you.
And I like them best when I am
Doing them with you.

(Sing to the polka tune 'Humperdinck')
With my hands I clap, clap, clap,
With my feet I tap, tap, tap,
Right foot first, left foot then,
Round the world and back again.

With my eyes I see, see, see,
With my ears I hear, hear, hear,
Right foot first, left foot then,
Round the world and back again.

Finger Plays and Rhymes

RHYMES

'Down at the station early in the morning' (*This Little Puffin*)

Chop and chip,
Chop and chip,
Cut down a tree
To build your ship.

Chip and chop,
Chip and chop,
Wait for the call
That tells you to stop.
Chip, chop, chip, chop,
Chip, chop . . .
TIMBER!

Rhythm Rhymes

Drama and movement

Play a Follow my Leader game. Each time make a sound and a movement for the children to copy.

Another story

Sheila and Bob had a bright idea. They bought a bird table and put it outside the kitchen window. It was like a little house on a pole. It had a thatched roof and a little round hole at the top, like a window to a bedroom up in the roof. They hung a special metal bird feeder from the bird table and filled it with nuts.

Every day Sheila and Bob watched the birds eating while they had their breakfast. They saw great tits, blue tits and nuthatches and, sometimes, a woodpecker. Robins and sparrows ate the bits which fell to the ground. They specially liked the nuthatches which ate upside down! After a week or two they noticed that some of the birds were pulling pieces of straw out of the thatched roof of the little house. At first they felt cross. Bob said, 'Why are they spoiling the lovely bird table we have given them?' Then he realized that they were using the straw to line their nests and he didn't feel so angry.

One day one of the blue tits popped through the hole in the little house into the tiny room under the roof. Soon she popped out again and fetched her mate. He also popped in to have a look. Over and over again they visited the little room. They were very careful. They always stopped and looked to and fro, to and fro, making sure that it was safe before they went in. They didn't realize that Sheila and Bob were watching them and wondering what was going to happen next.

One day Sheila noticed that the blue tits were doing something different. They were taking tiny twigs and bits of straw from the roof into the tiny house. They were making a nest! Day after day they worked hard and continued to pop in and out.

Some time later Bob noticed that one of the blue tits had something different in its beak. 'Look,' he said, 'I think there are baby blue tits in the nest, and they're feeding them.' Bob and Sheila were very excited and watched very carefully. They thought there must be babies in the nest. But how could they be sure? The hole was much too small to see through and they didn't want to frighten the birds. Then Sheila had an idea. 'If there are babies in the nest they will be making a noise,' she said. 'Hungry baby birds always do.' When the father and mother birds had flown off to look for food she crept quietly up to the bird table. Sure enough, she could hear tiny squeaking noises. The room in the little house was full of baby birds.

One day Bob saw a fluffy baby bird peering out of the hole. He knew it was getting ready to fly. He went off to work, but as soon as he and Sheila came back home they went to the window to watch the birds. They watched and watched. Nothing happened. They went outside to listen. All was quiet. There were no tiny noises, no fluffy babies, no parent birds flying in and out of the nest. While they were out all the birds had flown! They felt quite sad, but, 'Never mind,' they said, 'perhaps the blue tits will come back again next year.' Do you think they will?

Story books

- *All Together Now*
- *Find Out About Light and Sound*
- *Hiding*
- *I Hear*
- *I See*
- *My First Look at Noises*
- *What Can Pinky Hear?*
- *What Can Pinky See?*

Worship time

Gather in a circle around a low table. On the table place a pottery goblet and plate (or simple chalice and paten). For prayer time look and listen for a short time in silence. Then ask someone to sing 'From hand to hand' (*BBP*) while everyone listens.

Smelling

Setting

On different tables in the room place some of the following:

FLOWERING THINGS

Branches of trees with scented blossom, bowls of hyacinths or other scented bulbs, vases of scented flowers.

VEGETABLES, HERBS AND FRUIT

Bunches of herbs. Onions, with and without skins, fresh tomatoes, leeks, okra, chillies, garlic and other vegetables. Different kinds of fruit to cut and smell.

DRINKS

Flasks of coffee, cocoa, Bovril or soup (not too hot). Pineapple juice, lemon juice, Coke, etc.

STRONG-SMELLING FOODS

Hot bread, curry, cheese, fish, etc.

HOUSEHOLD ITEMS

Pot pourri, bath salts (and warm water), perfumes, essential oils, moth balls, soap, linament (Vicks), polish, incense sticks.

UNPLEASANT SMELLS

Manure, dried blood and bone fertilizer, or other unpleasant smells.

Put a selection of these (or others) into small fabric bags so that the children can guess the contents from the smell.

Sharing

What is your favourite smell? What smells do you not like? What smells do you smell out of doors? What part of your body helps you to smell?

Allow the children to smell and look at all the things in the setting. How many of them can they identify? Can they guess the smells in the fabric bags?

Bible story
JOHN 21.1–14

'Come on, what's the point of sitting around here being miserable? It's a good day for fishing. Who's coming with me?' Peter got up, and some of the other friends who were feeling sad because they were missing Jesus decided to go with him. They fished all the afternoon and all night, but they did not catch anything. When the sun rose they decided to row back to the shore. Nothing was going right.

As they got near the land they could just see someone standing there beside a little fire. He called out, 'Have you any fish?' Peter replied, 'Not this time, so we're coming in.' Then the man on the shore said 'Put your nets over the other side of the boat.'

The men thought this was a silly idea. 'We've been out here for hours and haven't caught any fish.' But Peter said, 'Let's have a go,' and soon the nets were full of fish.

'Thank you very much, whoever you are,' shouted Thomas. 'I know who it is,' said John. 'It's Jesus! Let's hurry up so we can see him.' 'Jesus?' said Peter. 'What's he doing here?' He was so excited he jumped out of the boat into the water and swam to the beach. As the rest of them rowed the boat nearer to the shore there was the delicious smell of bread. 'Bring some fish to cook,' said Jesus. 'And we'll all have breakfast together.' Everyone said the smell of the fish cooking was making them really hungry. Soon they were enjoying breakfast. 'This is one breakfast we'll never forget,' said the disciples to each other. 'I shall remember it each time I smell fish and bread cooking,' said John.

Activities

- Depending upon your location, go on a walk which has interesting scents!
- Make and bake bread, bake part-baked bread or use a bread mix (see recipe in Appendix, page 106).

- Provide the ingredients for the children to make sardines on toast.
- Make banana sandwiches or milkshakes.
- Polish the furniture with a strong-smelling polish.
- For gifts for Mothering Sunday, etc. provide small plastic bottles (e.g. from Body Shop), large inexpensive containers of bubble bath liquid and funnels. Children can then fill their own container and stick a picture on to it, cut from a seed magazine or taken from a sheet of stickers.

Music and rhymes

SONGS

'Jesus called to Peter the fisherman' (*BBP*)

'All things bright and beautiful' (Traditional)

'London's burning' (Traditional)

Sail, sail your fishing boat
Out across the sea.
Wave, wave, to the man
On the beach at Galilee.

Throw, throw, throw your nets
Throw them in the sea.
Pull, pull, pull them in.
Fish from Galilee.

Cook, cook, cook the fish
Caught freshly from the sea –
Breakfast with Jesus
On the beach at Galilee.
(*Sing to the tune of 'Row, row, row your boat'*)

Let's Praise and Pray

I jump out of bed in the morning (x3)
And my nose is ready to smell.

I soap myself all over (x3)
Oh, what an interesting smell.

I clean my teeth with toothpaste (x3)

Oh, what an interesting smell.
Other ideas:
We cook the toast for breakfast
We make a drink for breakfast
We clean our shoes with polish
We cut the grass in the garden, etc.

(*Sing to the tune of 'I jump out of bed in the morning'*)

Traditional, in *Okki Tokki Unga*

RHYMES

What is that smell
Coming up the stair?
Someone's making coffee
So I'll soon be there.

What is that smell
Coming from next door?
Someone's lit a bonfire,
It's against the law!

What is that smell
Coming from that shop?
It's an Indian curry,
Mummy, can we stop?

What is that smell
Coming from the road?
Someone's spreading tar
A steaming, gleaming load.

What is that smell
Coming from the sea?
Someone's caught some shellfish
I'd love some for my tea.

Drama and movement

- Act out the story of Jesus by the seashore, and eat the sardines on toast.
- Pretend to have a barbecue, preparing, cooking and eating the food, smelling all the time.

Another story

'How long before we go?' asked Sarah. She was very excited. She was going to visit her cousin Alan and then he was coming to visit her. He lived a long way away, so they didn't see each other very often. Sarah's mother told her that Alan didn't live in a big town, where there were busy roads and lots of shops and houses, like her town. His house was out in the country by itself and there were no shops nearby.

They packed the car with Sarah's luggage. They were soon at Alan's house. Alan was waiting for them and Sarah asked him straightaway where he went for walks and what he could see on them. Alan said there was plenty to see but his favourite walk was the one with the different smells.

'Smells!' said Sarah. 'What smells?' Alan said, 'Wait and see.' Sarah was so surprised she could hardly wait to set out. Sarah's mother said she would go with the two children on the walk.

At first the walk was along a footpath beside a high hedge that was covered with little white flowers. They smelt lovely. A bit further on there was a different smell. Sarah asked Alan, 'What is that smell?' 'There are horses the other side of the hedge,' he said. 'It's not like the flowers, is it, although it's quite nice, but just wait until we get near the farm. There is an awful smell when the cowshed has just been cleaned – the farmer calls it mucking out.' He was right. Sarah and her mother decided to hold their noses! The farmer saw them and laughed. 'Come in this shed and see the little lambs – their woolly coats have another different smell.'

Then on the way back to Alan's house they passed a bank of bluebells and primroses – a good smell this time. As they got to Alan's door, they could smell freshly baked cakes. Sarah couldn't get her hands washed quickly enough because she was hungry and the tea smelt great.

On the way home Sarah wondered if there was a walk with different smells she could take Alan on when he came to visit her in the town. Mummy said, 'Tomorrow we will go on a "discovering smells" walk.'

Next day they set out along the busy road. There was the smell that came from all the cars, which they didn't like very much. But then there was the bread shop, the fish and chip shop and the shop where Sarah's mother bought her coffee. The smells there were all different but they were nice. As they got near the corner Sarah and her mother both started sniffing – now what was that smell? When they turned the corner there was a big machine spreading hot black tar on the road. They both decided they liked that smell. 'I hope that's still there when Alan comes,' said Sarah. 'Then we'll have an interesting walk of smells for him, but I'm glad some of them are different. Isn't it fun going on smelly walks?'

Story books

- *The Smelly Book* (*The last section is less suitable for younger children.*)
- *Who's Making That Smell?*

Worship time

Light a scented candle. Ask the children to choose something from the setting of which they like the smell. Thank God for the wonders of creation and in particular for the different smells chosen by the children.

NOTE

This theme would be particularly suitable in Spring or early Summer. Sensitivity will be required when talking about unpleasant smells as children can be very frank.

Appendix

Shoe and boot printing

Provide a wide variety of shoes and boots with interesting soles including football boots.

Cover the floor with plastic or shower curtains or work outside.

Place pieces of foam sheeting in the bottom of a large baking tin or litter tray.

Cover the foam with bright coloured paint.

Place at one end of long sheet of lining paper or similar. At the other end place a large bowl of clean soapy water and some drying cloths.

Card weaving

Cards should be pre-prepared with notches and wool warp pre-wound.

Use a piece of firm card 15 cm x 10 cm.

Cut V shapes in the card approx. 2 cm apart at both ends of the card.

Wind wool for warp up and down the notches.

Use thick wool in large blunt bodkins for the weaving.

Knot the wool for the start and encourage in and out weaving.

Modelling dough that bakes solid (salt dough)

Use: 250 g plain flour, 200 g salt, 1 tsp glycerine, 350 ml lukewarm water.

Mix flour, salt and glycerine. Gradually add enough water to knead into a flexible dough.

Model with it

Put on a baking tray.

Bake in preheated oven at Gas mark 1 or 140 °C, 275 °F for two hours or until dough is dry right through.

Alternatively cook slowly in the microwave, usually on low or medium power, allowing the shapes to rest and cool on a cooling rack between times to prevent overcooking and bubbling.

Paint and varnish the dried shapes to preserve the dough.

Biscuit recipe

Use: 225 g plain flour, 55 g butter, 30 g sugar, 1 tsp baking powder, a pinch of salt, 150 ml milk.

Mix all ingredients together thoroughly to form a dough.

Roll out on lightly floured surface and cut into small rounds with a cutter.

Place on baking tray in a preheated oven and bake at Gas mark 7 or 220 °C, 425 °F for about 15 minutes.

Leave to rest for one minute before transferring to the cooling rack.

Stretchy modelling dough

Use: 1¹/₂ kg self-raising flour, 3 dsps powder paint if desired, water (approx. 650 ml).

Work it well to make it stretchy.

Quick bread dough

Use: 1 packet yeast (approx 13 g), 250 ml warm water and milk, 250 g molasses, 250 g wholemeal flour, 250 g strong white flour, 2 tsp salt, 25 g butter.

Grease the tins for either bread or rolls.

Blend yeast with 2 tbsps water and milk.

Dissolve the molasses in the remaining water and milk.

Sift flour and salt into a bowl and rub in the butter.

Make well in centre and add the yeast liquid and the molasses liquid and mix to a soft dough.

Turn on to a floured surface and knead for 8 minutes until the dough is smooth and elastic.

Shape the dough as rolls or loaves and put on or in tins.

Place the tins in greased polythene bags and leave to rise in a warm place, until the dough is twice the size.

Remove from the bag and bake in a hot oven 200 °C for 5–15 min depending on size.

Always cool on a wire tray.

Coleslaw

1 small white cabbage shredded or finely sliced, 4 small carrots shredded, 1 onion sliced, enough yoghurt or fromage frais to bind together.

Mix all together and stir well.

Bubble painting

Put some paint in yoghurt pots and add washing-up liquid.

Place large sheets of shiny surface paper rather than sugar paper on tables.

Encourage the children to hold the pots over the paper. Put straws into the pots and blow the paint mixture until the bubbles tumble out of the pot on to the paper. The pots should be upright and the children should move the pots over the paper.

Blow painting

Use shiny paper.

Drop paint on to it with a thick brush.

With a straw blow the paint, either from above or sideways to form interesting patterns.

Resources

Story books

A Day Out, Leila Berg, Macmillan, 1968

The Aircraft, Gerard Browne, Orchard Books, 1992

Alfie Gets in First, Shirley Hughes, Bodley Head, 1991

Alfie Gives a Hand, Shirley Hughes, Bodley Head, 1981

Alfie's Feet, Shirley Hughes, Bodley Head, 1981

All Together Now, Nick Butterworth, Picture Lion, 1997

Anna Goes to School, Katie Teague, Magi, 1991

At School, Puffin, 1970

Bathwater's Hot, Shirley Hughes, Walker Books, 1985

Big Book of Noah's Ark, Stacie Strong, International Books, 1992

Book of Lullabies, Belinda Holyer and Robin Corfield, Bloomsbury, 1998

Boots for a Bridesmaid, Verna Wilkins, Tamarind, 1995

The Brave Ones, Tony Kerins, Walker Books, 1996

Bread, Judith Baskerville, Black, 1991

Bread, Kevin Rasher, Wayland, 1990

The Bridesmaid, Jean Strachan, Storychair, 1971

Can I Help? Marilyn Janovitz, North South Books, 1996

Can't You Sleep Little Bear?, Martin Waddell and Barbara Firth, Walker Books, 1998

Cars, Anne Rockwell, Puffin, 1998

Crystal and Gem, Louise Pritchard, Dorling Kindersley, 1991

Find Out About Light and Sound, David Palmer, BBC Education, 1994

Find Out About Light, David Palmer, BBC Education, 1994

Flowers, Claude Delafosse and Rene Mettler, Moonlight, 1992

Flowers, Jennifer Coldrey, HarperCollins, 1994

Getting Dressed, Kati Teague, Magi, 1989

Harry the Dirty Dog, Gene Zion, Bodley Head, 1960

Hello Goodbye, David Lloyd and Louise Voce, Walker Books, 1989

Hiding, Shirley Hughes, Walker Books, 1995

Holes and Peeks, Ann Jones, Walker Books, 1984

How a Zoo Works, Dinosaur, 1983

How the Zebra Got Its Stripes, Wildlife Clubs of Kenya, Hutchinson, 1978

I Don't Want To, Sally Grindley and Carol Thompson, Methuen, 1990

I Hear, Rachel Isadora, Puffin, 1985

I See, Rachel Isadora, Puffin, 1985

I Won't Go There Again, Susan Hill, MacRae Books, 1990

Impo, Jon Blake and Arthur Robius, Walker Books, 1992

Jill the Farmer's Wife and Friends, Nick Butterworth, Walker Books, 1991

Jingle Bells, Nick Butterworth, HarperCollins, 1998

The Jolly Postman, Janet and Alan Ahlberg, Guild, 1989

Katie Morag and the Wedding, Mairi Hedderwick, Red Fox, 1995

Let's All Dig and Burrow, Anna Nilsen and Anna Axworthy, Zero To Ten, 1997

Let's Look at Flowers, Nicola Tuxworth, Lorenz Books, 1996

Let's Look at Kitchens, Nicola Tuxworth, Lorenz Books, 1997

Let's Look at Kitchens, Nicola Tuxworth, Lorenz Books, 1997

Let's Look at People at Work, Ladybird, 1995

Let's Look at Things That Go, Nicola Tuxworth, Lorenz Books, 1998

Letters, Leila Berg, Macmillan, 1970

The Lighthouse Keeper's Catastrophe, Ronda and David Armitage, Scholastic, 1998

Lights, Leslie Francis and Nicola Slee, NCEC, 1997

Lights for Gita, Rachma Gilmore, Second Story Press, 1996

Lucy and Tom at the Seaside, Shirley Hughes, Puffin, 1993

Lucy and Tom Go to School, Shirley Hughes, Puffin, 1998

Lucy and Tom's ABC, Shirley Hughes, Puffin, 1984

Magic Beach, Alison Lester, Allen and Unwin, 1996

Mole in a Hole, Christina Butler, Simon and Schuster, 1993

Morton Gets Set, Karen Ludlow and Willy Smax, Orion, 1996

Moving House, Camilla Jessel, Methuen, 1981

Moving Molly, Shirley Hughes, Random Century, 1978

Mr Gumpy's Motor Car, John Burningham, Puffin, 1979

Mrs Armitage on Wheels, Quentin Blake, Picture Lion, 1990

My Bike, Ginn Science, 1989

My Dad Is Brilliant, Nick Butterworth, Walker Books, 1989

My Dad Is Wizard, Zero To Ten, 1998

My First Look at Noises, Jan Yorke, Dorling Kindersley, 1991

My First Look at Touch, Jane Yorke, Dorling Kindersley, 1990

My Gran Is Great, Zero To Ten, 1998

My Mum Is Magic, Zero To Ten, 1998

My Sister Is Super, Zero To Ten, 1998

Noisy, Shirley Hughes, Walker Books, 1985

Noisy Poems, Jill Bennett, OUP, 1987

Oliver's Wood, Sue Hendra, Walker Books, 1996

Owl Babies, Martin Waddell, Walker Books, 1992

The Pebble in My Pocket, Meredith Hooper, Lincoln, 1996

Rocks and Minerals, Janice Laycock, Dorling Kindersley, 1988

Sebastian's Trumpet, Mike Imai, Walker Books, 1996

See for Yourself: Sun, Kay Davies and Wendy Oldfield, Black, 1994

Shine a Light, Leslie Francis and Nicola Slee, NCEC, 1996

Shoes, Debbie Bailey, Annick Press, 1991

The Smallest Whale, Elizabeth Beresford, Orchard Books, 1998

The Smelly Book, Babette Cole, Picture Lion, 1990

The Snow Lady, Shirley Hughes, Walker Books, 1990

Sonny's Wonderful Wellies, Lisa Stubbs, Picadilly Press, 1997

Spot Goes to School, Eric Hill, Puffin, 1987

Spot's Touch and Feel Book, Eric Hill, Warne, 1997

Sunflowers, Philip Barker, Puffin, 1988

Sun's Hot – Sea's Cold, Paul Humphrey, Evans, 1993

The Surprise Party, Pat Hutchins, Puffin, 1969

Tales from Henry's Garden: Rumbles the Roller, Simon Hickes, Chart Books, 1995

There Yet?, Verna Watkins, Tamarind, 1995

There's a Dragon in My School, Jenny Tyler and Philip Hawthorn, Walker Books

This Is the Star, Joyce Dunbar and Gary Blythe, Doubleday, 1996

Toddlerobics, Zita Newcombe, Walker Books, 1991

Topsy and Tim Meet the Firefighters, Jean and Gareth Adamson, Ladybird, 1998

Touch, Mandy Suhr, Wayland, 1993

Touch and Feel Wild Animals, Dorling Kindersley, 1998

The Trouble with Grandad, Babette Cole, Mammoth, 1989

The Trunk, Brian Wildsmith, OUP, 1982

Two Shoes, New Shoes, Shirley Hughes, Walker Books, 1986

Vegetables, Kevin Rasher, Wayland, 1990

The Wedding Tea, Mary Cockett, Macmillan, 1970

The Whale's Story, Dyan Sheldon and Gary Blythe, Red Fox, 1993

What Can Pinky Hear?, Lucy Cousins, Walker Books, 1991

What Is the Sun, Walker Books, 1995

Whatever Next, Jill Murphy, Macmillan, 1995

Who's in Holes?, Richard Armour, Worlds Work, 1971

Who's Making That Smell?, Philip Hawthorne and Jenny Tyler, Usborne, 1995

Whose Shoes, Brian Wildsmith, OUP, 1984

Why Do Sunflowers Face the Sun?, Terry Martin, Dorling Kindersley, 1996

Music and rhymes books

Apusskidu, A. & C. Black, 1975

Carol, Gaily Carol, Beatrice Harrop (comp.), A. & C. Black, 1973

Come Follow Me, Elizabeth Gould, Evans, 1956, 1966

Finger Plays and Rhymes, Harrow Pre-School Playgroups Association, 1976

Happy Landings, Howard Sergeant (comp.), Evans, 1971

Helter Skelter, Alison Winn, Brockhampton Press Ltd, 1966

Knock at the Door, Jan Betts, Ward Lock Education, 1980

Let's Praise and Pray, Sheila Clift, Scripture Union, 1994

Mango Spice, Yvonne Conelly, Gloria Cameron and Sonia Singham (comp.), A. & C. Black, 1981

More Word Play, Finger Play, Pre-School Playgroups Association, 1985

Okki Tokki Unga, Beatrice Harrop, A & C Black, 1976

Rhythm Rhymes, Ruth Sansom, A.& C. Black, 1964

Sense and Nonsense: Listening, Susanne Shona McKellar (comp.), Macdonald, 1985

Speech Rhymes, Clive Sansom, A.& C. Black, 1974

Someone's Singing, Lord, A. & C. Black, 1973

Story Song, Stainer & Bell and the Methodist Division of Education &a Youth, 1973

Ta-ra-boom-de-ay, David Gadsby and Beatrice Harrop (comp), A. & C. Black, 1977

Tinderbox, A. & C. Black, 1982

A Word in Season, Donald Hilton (comp.), NCEC, 1984

Word Play, Finger Play, Pre-School Playgroups Association, 1985

Bible Index